Faith A. Oyedepo

The Effective Minister's Wife

THE EFFECTIVE MINISTER'S WIFE

Faith A. Oyedepo

ISBN 978-2905-46-1

2nd Print: June 2008

Published in Nigeria by:

DOMINION PUBLISHING HOUSE

DOMINION PUBLISHING HOUSE

Faith Tabernacle, Km 10, Idiroko Road,

Canaan Land, Ota.

Tel: 234-1-7747546, 7747547, 7747548.

Websites: www.davidoyedepoministries.org

www.domistores.org

All Scriptures are from the King James Version of the Bible, except otherwise stated.

Contents

Dedication

To Dr. David Olaniyi Oyedepo

By divine arrangement, we met over thirty one years ago and got married over twenty five years ago.

Then I could not have imagined that God would do all that He is doing in our lives and ministry.

Getting married to you has privileged me to be a minister's wife.

To God and you I am eternally grateful.

I love you with passion.

Introduction

You are married to a minister of the gospel, what an honour! To be the wife of your pastor, shepherd and most importantly God's servant is to say the least an enviable privilege. God carefully "selected" you among an uncountable number of eligible women to be the companion of His called one, to be by his side in carrying out his God-given assignment. You are a woman on a God-ordained mission and you are very special indeed.

To be sure, yours is an assignment that is not only enviable and rewarding but also very demanding, very tasking and one that requires great focus and determination. Like every other vocation and career in life, your assignment is not without its peculiar challenges. This explains why for the most part, many ministers' wives are simply living frustrated lives from day to day. Life has become a drudgery of some sort as they grapple with the incessant demands of ministry life for which sadly, many of them are not fully prepared or are not willing to even embrace.

More often than not, the congregation or the people

that you are sent to also offer very little respite to ministers of the gospel in general and ministers' wives in particular. The people place you on a pedestal in their minds because they already have a set mould of what a minister's wife should be (some reasonable and scriptural, others downright unrealistic and unattainable), and they hold that standard up and judge you by it most of the time.

Painfully too, in some cases some ministers of the gospel themselves are not well informed about their wives' roles in their lives and ministries. This lack of knowledge often translates into strained relationship at home, which in turn impacts negatively upon the work of the ministry entrusted into their hands.

You hold in your hands a book written by a minister's wife for ministers' wives bearing in mind the above all-too-familiar scenario. Whether your husband is called to be an apostle, prophet, pastor, evangelist or teacher; or helps any of the above to fulfil their mission, God has called you as his wife to be by his side and to function effectively at your assignment. It is one thing to be called and it is another thing entirely to be effective and to make a difference.

If you happen to be an informed minister's wife who is already making a difference in your husband's life and ministry, there are higher heights yet as your level of effectiveness can be enhanced and improved upon. Proverbs 4:18 says: *But the path of the just is like the shinning light that shinneth more and more unto the perfect day.*

Remember, someone said, "The largest room in the world is the room for improvement."

Hebrews 6:12 also says: *but be followers of them who through faith and patience inherit the promises.*

I have the privilege of being involved in the work of the ministry with my husband for over twenty-five years running. In this book I share heart-to-heart with you as my highly esteemed fellow co-labourer some of the truths that have helped me till date. These are truths that I have proved and that I still walk in up till today. The truth is that I am not perfect neither have I arrived yet. I am still learning and striving to be a more effective minister's wife.

Like me, may you resolve after reading this book to explore to the fullest all of the rich deposits of God on your inside meant to add to the work of the ministry in your husband's care. May this book not only answer some of your questions but also be a source of the much-needed encouragement and inspiration to spur you to unimaginable heights alongside your husband.

Together, may we hear from our Lord when we stand before Him at the end of our journey here; "well done good and faithful servant, enter into the rest of your Lord."

Go, my friend, the best lies ahead!

Chapter 1

The Minister, His Wife And The Ministry

Who Is A Minister?

The *American Heritage Dictionary* defines a minister as: *"A person serving as an agent for another by carrying out specified orders or functions."*

To "minister" means to render active help or service to someone or something. Service entails working for another person with the aim of assisting in the performance of a task and hastening its completion. Thus, a minister is a person who renders a service to another, towards the performance of a task. The same is true of a minister of the gospel.

In the context of the gospel of the kingdom of God, the task or assignment is the ministry. The duties executed by a person to fulfill this task are the work of the ministry.

...And he gave gifts to men.

...he gave some, apostles, and some, prophets, and some evangelists, and some, pastors and teachers.

For the perfecting of the saints, for the work of the ministry for the edifying of the body of Christ:

till we all come in the unity of the faith and of the knowledge of the son of God unto a perfect man, unto the measure of the stature of the fullness of Christ.

Ephesians 4:8, 11-13

From the above scripture therefore, a minister of the gospel is one who does, either directly or indirectly; the work of the ministry towards the church of Christ by performing the duties of any of the ministry offices mentioned above. It is important to note that such people are representatives of Christ in the governing of His body.

These ministers who themselves are gifts of God to men, are divinely enabled with gifts by the Holy Spirit to work alongside Christ in the building up of his body to maturity. As Paul the apostle said, "we, then, as workers together with him ...are labourers together with God ..." (2 Corinthians 6:1; 1 Corinthians 3:9).

For each office there is a particular duty to be performed as well as particular tools to carry out these duties. Paul the apostle said *"...for in nothing am I behind the very chiefest apostle, though I be nothing. Truly the signs of an apostle were wrought among you..."* (2 Corinthians 12:11-12).

So, someone who serves in the office of either an apostle, or prophet, or evangelist, or pastor or teacher or who helps any of the above to fulfill his commission is a minister of God and is doing some service of a kind for Christ towards the edification and governing of his body on earth.

"...the ***work*** *of the MINISTRY..."* in Ephesians chapter 4 means that MINISTRY is "work". Ministry is all about imparting lives with the gospel. Every minister must desire that as he does "the work of the ministry", lives of men be imparted with the gospel. Ministry is not in titles (even though titles are biblical, necessary and important), it is work. As a minister, ask yourself how much you are investing in the work of the ministry.

Concern yourself primarily with the "work" dimension of ministry, instead of being only title- conscious. Titles become relevant, only when the work dimension of ministry is applied. God rewards work, not titles and only labourers not supervisors are worthy of wages (Luke 10:7)!

Who Is A Minister's Wife?

In Genesis (the beginning of beginnings), God made man (Genesis 2:7), gave him an assignment (Genesis 2:15) and then made the woman as a helpmeet, to make up for that which was lacking in the man; a suitable assistant to him in the completion of his God-given task (Genesis.2:18). A minister has an assignment from the Lord.

Likewise a minister's wife is one who is married to a man who operates directly or indirectly in any of the five – fold ministry offices. She is a wife of an apostle, a prophet, an evangelist, a pastor, a teacher, a deacon, an elder, a bishop, or anyone who helps someone in the five-fold ministry to fulfill the great commission.

She assists her husband in his God –given task and thus is also a co-minister in the divine task given to him. Even though titles are good and scriptural, she does not necessarily have to bear titles like deaconess, pastor, evangelist etc. before she can be effective as a minister's wife. In actual fact, she is a co-minister alongside her husband.

As a wife, she is meant to assist her husband in the work of the ministry IN EVERY WAY POSSIBLE. She has a lot to do with how effectively the minister, who is her husband, performs his duties.

Truly, beside every successful man is a successful woman as well! The importance of her co-operation – spirit, soul and body cannot be overemphasized and is needed by her husband to ensure a successful ministry.

The scripture makes us understand that to be married in Christ is a gift, ... *God gives some the gift of a husband or wife...* (1Corinthians 7: 7 TLB). However, when talking about the single and married it says, let every man abide in the same CALLING wherein he was CALLED (1Corinthians 7:20).

Being a minister's wife is a calling in itself. It is a calling from God, not from man. It is important to understand at this point that it is not just a calling but also a HIGH CALLING. The scripture *says: I press toward the m*ark for the prize of the high calling of God in Christ Jesus (Philippians 3:14). As a minister's wife, there are certain things you must take note of in the above scripture.

It Is A High Calling

First, being a minister's wife is a calling. A calling is a divine commission, assignment or placement. It is not a position of merit. You became a minister's wife, not by accident, coincidence or luck, but by God's divine placement. It is an enviable position and there are many women who wish they were you; married to a minister.

How fortunate you are! It is not just a calling, but also a high calling.

It will be absurd of you as a minister's wife for instance to think that life would have been better for you, if you were not a minister's wife. I can assure you, it would have been worse! You must understand that you are highly favoured by God. See God's HIGH calling upon your life and embrace it!

My husband, Dr. David Oyedepo has said, "inferiority complex is the bait of failure." Don't ever belittle or look down on yourself, no matter what is happening around you. Whatever challenges you are facing right now as a minister's wife, are not beyond you by virtue of the divine deposits inside you. See yourself overcoming that challenge with the eyes of faith and you will surely overcome.

How you see your calling determines your perspective which in turn will affect your level of interest and ultimately the level of impact you make. It will also subsequently determine the blessings you receive as you faithfully walk in this high calling.

In Genesis 3:14-15, the scripture says: *lift up now thine eyes ... all the land which thou seest, to thee will I give it...*" It is only what you see with the eyes of your mind that God will give to you. How do you see your being a minister's wife? Do you see it as a burden or a blessing? Do you see it as a privilege or just as pass time? Remember, what you see is what you get!

Your mind is the pace setter of your destiny. Being a minister's wife is a HIGH calling: SEE it that way, and then you will attain that GREAT height that God has prepared for you.

It Is Of God

> ***...high calling OF GOD in Christ Jesus***
>
> Philippians 3:14.

Next, your being a minister's wife is not just a high calling, it is also of God .You did not get married to a minister by mistake or coincidence. It is of God and because it is of God, it means it is from God. It is not man who made you a minister's wife but God Himself.

"I never bargained for this!" someone may say. Yes, you did not bargain for it and probably you believe it is even a mistake for you to have become a minister's wife. But you know what; God can turn the mistakes of your life into an outstanding miracle, if you let Him! Don't be carried away by the lie of your enemy, the devil; remember that he is a liar, deceiver and thief. Do not let his steal your joy and fulfillment.

Yes - you had your own plans that were completely different from what obtains now, but remember that God's ways and thoughts are higher than yours (Isaiah 55:9); but it is all for your good! Refuse to be trapped by the devil. It is not too late for you to have the best life that you can possibly have. So, rejoice, grab the opportunity with both hands and be the best.

An understanding of this will make you seek to please God who has divinely called and placed you. Since you are divinely called, handle the call faithfully. Don't render eye service but heart service. This is where many people miss it in ministry. Even if your minister husband is serving under a ministry, seek to please God primarily as His servant and then it will become easy for your superiors to be pleased with you.

Until God is pleased with you, even if man is pleased with you it holds no lasting reward. When God is pleased with you, He will cause men to be pleased with you and you also enjoy lasting rewards. You would not need to struggle to 'buy' favour from your boss or superiors if you seek to please God, it will come to you without sweat.

In the same vein, as a minister's wife, your calling is of God; so seek to please Him first. As you do this, He will make life pleasurable for you.

The Prize

I press toward the mark for the prize ...

Philippians 3:14.

God is a faithful rewarder. He does not only call, He also gives prizes. Isn't that awesome?

There is both temporal (earthly) and eternal (heavenly) prize for every calling that is successfully pursued. Here on earth, the prize may come in form of monetary or material rewards or it may come in form of things that money cannot buy such as peace, fulfillment, long life, divine health, prosperity, joy and so on.

Eternally, it comes in form of Jesus' commendation, "...well done, good and faithful servant..." (Matthew 25:23); or to sit with Him on His throne (Revelations 3: 21); or to rule (Matthew 25: 21). May you not miss your prize and may another not take your prize! Many men-ministers have missed their prizes because of the kind of wives they got married to. May you not be one of such!

Interestingly, as a minister's wife, you are meant to receive both temporal and eternal prizes. You must understand, however that it is one thing to be called but another thing entirely to receive the prize. Not all that are called automatically receive the prize.

You must take conscious, deliberate and practical steps to fulfill the call before you can receive the prize. Let no one take your place or prize because prizes are transferable in the kingdom of God!

Focus on God however, not on the prize; and serve God with all intent and purpose. For over twenty-five (25) years that I have been privileged to be a minister's wife, God and how to please Him has always been my focus; not the prize. Do not serve God because of the prize but because of who He is. The prize should not be your motivation in ministry. God should be.

Those who are in ministry for what to gain never amount to much and usually end up as losers; but those who are there to serve God always win and have a story to tell! The choice is yours. That is why I have a story to tell today!

Plus, I am presently enjoying some level of rewards. I am confident I will not lose my prize for anything. Like me, you too can resolve to serve God faithfully and you will surely lay hold on the prize.

Assuredly, your investment and labour in the pursuit of God's calling upon your life will not go unrewarded! However, there is what you must do before you can receive the prize; and this takes us to the next point.

Press Toward The Mark

> ***I press toward the mark...***
>
> Phillipians3: 14

Before you can receive the prize however, you must be ready to press. Pressing here does not refer to exerting physical energy or effort. The living Bible says: *...I strain to reach the end of the race...*

To 'strain' means to stretch, to pull, to put pressure of something. It means consciously putting aside every impediment on your way and doggedly pursuing your assignment to the very end. Please be aware, being a minister's wife is not a journey of convenience!

The Bible says:

> ***...like an athlete I punish my body... training it to do what it should, not what it wants to...***
>
> 1 Corinthians 9: 27

Just like an athlete, you require a lot of personal training which involves putting the body under subjection. You know what? Never make personal comfort your priority, if you desire to be effective as a minister's wife! You must be ready to function beyond the comfort zone of life.

It is of utmost importance for you also to *...lay aside every weight and sin that easily besets thee so you may* *run with patience the race...* (Hebrews 12:1). This means you must get rid of sins and weights in order to 'press' successfully.

Clearly, every unrighteousness is sin (I John 5: 17). What are weights? You may ask. They are things which in themselves may not be sinful per se, but which can hinder your progress and pressing forward.

These may be seemingly minor issues such as: too much time spent watching television instead of studying the word, unnecessary visits instead of praying and getting more acquainted with the presence of God, excessive sleep rather than investing such time in something more productive, or things like that.

Remember that Apostle Paul said: *All things are LAWFUL but not all things are EXPEDIENT for me...* (1Corinthians 6:12) or as the living Bible says: *...not all things are helpful...* You must choose the 'expedient' above the 'lawful'. The 'lawful' is what is not sinful, what is allowed. On the other hand, the 'expedient' is what is helpful, useful and profitable. You must begin to function beyond the level of what is allowed to the level of what is helpful, useful and profitable.

But, "how" you may ask, "can I actually press, since pressing in this context does not connote physical exertion?" As a minister's wife who desires to receive the prize, consider the following avenues:

In-Depth Word Study

> ***Study to show thyself approved unto God, a workman that needeth not to be ashamed, rightly dividing the word of truth.***
>
> 2 Timothy 2:15

It is really very important for you to be studious as a minister's wife. Learn to bend down to study the word of God regularly and apply it to your day-to-day living.

Read, study, meditate and live the word! Until you begin to live the word, you cannot affect your world. And remember, you cannot be a leader except you are a reader.

This responsibility cannot be transferred to anyone, not even to your minister husband. In the same vein, the studious life of your minister husband can neither be transferred nor imparted to you! As a minister's wife, your depth in the word of God determines your height in life and ministry. How long you have been a minister's wife is not as important as how much depth you have.

The word of God that you take in is what provides you with the strength and stamina for the race of the ministry, which can actually be very tasking and demanding most times; to say the least.

Personally, I take my word study time very seriously. I actually esteem it higher than my physical food. Many years ago, I resolved in my heart that consistent daily word study for living; not for preaching, takes priority in my life. And I can tell you this, it pays!

Keep in mind the fact that ministry is basically dealing with the devil, your adversary. This requires you carrying the presence of God with you all of the time. The only way for this to be possible is for you to constantly spend personal, private, quality fellowship time with God. Your private word study time is even far more important than the time you spend in public meetings.

Refuse every form of distraction and establish a quality relationship with God. This is what ultimately determines your rating and relevance. Understand that you can always draw strength and be empowered through your union with God. (Ephesians 6:10-11)

The truth is that there is no substitute for a studious life, if you want to be an effective minister's wife. God desires to have a relationship with you. So, dissociate from religion and embrace a life of fruitful relationship with God. If you do not want to be ashamed, study! Give priority importance to this and the difference will be clear in your life, plus; you will have results to show.

Heart-felt Prayer

> ***But we will give ourselves continually to prayer, and to the ministry of the word.***
>
> Acts 6:4

You must be prayerful. Consistent heart-felt prayer as a lifestyle enlivens your spirit, keeps you spiritually on fire and enhances your effectiveness.

Over the years I have become aware that nothing is either too small or too big to pray about. Prayer is synonymous with power. To be prayerless is to be powerless. The more prayerful you are the more spiritual power you are able to exercise. Heart-felt prayer always produces undeniable proofs (Acts 4: 23).

Prayer is one of your greatest assets as a minister's wife. It is not optional but mandatory if you desire to be effective. Never get to a point where your prayer life begins to drag. This could be very dangerous as it could be a sign that you are getting farther from God. And you know; this could expose you to the wickedness of your adversary, the devil. It could result in continuous struggle in life as well as unending breakdowns!

Wake up! Refuse to fold your hands at the opposition through prayerlessness! You cannot afford to sit down there crying at situations and circumstances, always waiting to be 'carried' spiritually by your minister husband; or for someone to pity you.

You are meant to be a blessing and a support to your husband, lifting his hands up as he carries out his God-given assignment; just like Aaron and Hur were to Moses (Exodus 17: 12). You are, and not a burden. You are not meant to be pitied because you are not in the pit; rather, you are to be envied. You will make it!

Prayer is actually your communication link with God, your heavenly father. It is a known fact that every strong relationship thrives on the maintenance of a good communication link between the parties involved; in the same vein, prayer enhances the strength of your relationship with God because it is one of the ways to fellowship with Him: plus, it is one of the means of getting God to intervene in your affairs. What a privilege!

Really, prayer is one of your covenant responsibilities (Luke 18: 1). When you fail in it, you never amount to much in life and ministry. But if you arise to this responsibility, you are the one to benefit.

Among other things, heart-felt prayer gives you access to help from above (Hebrews 4: 16); which you as a minister's wife need more than anything else. If you must enjoy deliverance from afflictions, which is uppermost, you must be armed with the weapon of prayer (James 5: 13).

With prayer, you are able to enforce biblical prophesies (I Timothy 1: 18), enjoy angelic intervention (Acts 12: 5- 11) and provoke mercy from God (2 Samuel 24: 14). It also enhances your level of consecration (Zechariah 3: 4) and helps you in locating the path of life (Psalm 23: 1, 5).

Your prayer must however be word-based, i.e. pray in line with the word of God concerning every issue. Learn to pray for your minister husband, family members and the work of the ministry at large.

For me, it is as crucial as the breath I take! Now, I come against every form of prayer weariness in your life and decree fresh oil upon you right now, in the mighty name of Jesus Christ! Beloved, the importance of this cannot be over-emphasized!

Diligent Kingdom Service

You cannot afford to be lazy if you want to press successfully. Don't just sit down there, just occupying space for nothing! Refuse to only watch things being done, be a part of getting them done! Diligence in the things of God and in service to the Lord is required. To press, you must be armed with diligence. No diligence, no pressing!

Seest thou a man diligent in his business? He shall stand before kings; he shall not stand before mean men.

Proverbs 22:29

Use your energy, intellect, position, possession, and all you are and have to serve God. Service is the master key to a fruitful life. When you serve God, He preserves your life. Refuse to be an idle minister's wife in the kingdom of God. After all, you are first and foremost a child of God before a minister's wife (how easy it is to forget that)!

Personally, I have been privileged to serve in various ways in the ministry. I remember when our ministry newly began; I was one of the volunteer cleaners of the church. I was once in the choir. I was a member of the first church decorating unit. At one time, I was a Bible study teacher. I had also served in the children's department: to mention a few – and all of these joyfully and with excitement!

Up till now, I still keep in touch with most of these groups in one way or another, making my little contributions there. Countless areas of service opportunities are at your disposal, right at your finger tips. Take advantage of them to enhance your effectiveness. Don't seek to be known, seek to serve!

Be a practical, hands-on person when it comes to using your talents, gifts and time in the service of your heavenly father. You occupy a very sensitive and important position. Be a functional joint in the body of Christ, supplying your own part to ensure the overall growth of the body (Ephesians 4: 4, 16).

Refuse to be a benchwarmer! Take action! Time is running out. As a minister's wife you have been planted on a most fruitful hill (Isaiah 5: 1-7). Consider this very seriously. But, are you bearing fruit or just cumbering the ground (Luke 13: 7–9)? God is seeking fruit of you. You shall not be cut down!

Invest into your destiny. God promises to spare those who serve Him (Malachi 3: 17-18). Whatever will compete with your service and devotion to God must be done away with. So, serve Him unreservedly- with gladness and not as a burden (Psalm 100:2; Jeremiah 23: 36, 38; Deuteronomy 28: 47-48), with a perfect heart (I Chronicles 28: 9), and continually (Daniel 6: 6). This is wisdom.

Diligent kingdom service attracts supernatural blessings (Exodus 23: 25; Psalms 75: 6-7; Proverbs 10:22), supernatural deliverances (Daniel 6: 16, 24; Exodus 32:10), and distinction in all areas of life (Malachi 3: 17; Exodus 23: 25-26); to name a few. I can tell you this: I am a beneficiary of all these and even more!

Locate where you belong in the kingdom and serve God faithfully there. Would you?

Hard-Core Faithfulness

You cannot press successfully without being faithful. Faithfulness is required in all that is committed into your hands. Be faithful, not face-full! Handle every assignment as unto the Lord, not as unto man. Constantly remember that God is watching!

One of the scriptures that have particularly been my guiding principles in life and in the work of the ministry as a pastor's wife, which I believe will be helpful to you as well is presented below:

> ***The eyes of the Lord are in every place, beholding the evil and the good.***
>
> Proverbs 15: 3

Faithfulness is the ladder to greatness. Faithfully do that which is committed to you without seeking commendation from men, not even your minister husband (I know this is difficult, especially when you are 'helping him out' with the work of the ministry).

Until you are faithful in that which God gave you as a minister's wife, He will not lift you or commit more into your hands. Woman, God's calling is upon your life! Press with diligent service. Don't involve yourself in the game of eye service like many do. Remember the word says:

> ***But with me it is a very small thing that I should be judged of you, or of man's judgement: yea, I judge not mine own self.***
>
> 1 Corinthians 4:3

Your calling is not from man, so seek to please the one who has called you- God Himself.

God's purpose concerning you is: *she will do him good and not evil all the days of her life* (Proverbs 31:12). There is a lot your husband cannot do effectively as a minister without your positive input, commitment and assistance. The significance of your role as it relates to the success of his ministry is of uttermost importance.

Don't ever feel insignificant or that you cannot play a major role in his affairs. Do not forget: ...*God hath chosen the weak things of the world to confound the wise and God hath chosen the weak things of the world to confound the things which are mighty* (1 Corinthians 1:27).

God saw you and all your 'inadequacies' even before you realized them. So, don't disqualify yourself! God knows and understands you more than you understand yourself (Psalms 139: 15-16). You are just perfect for your God-ordained assignment!

The call of God is not by merit and cannot be obtained by works for He says: *For ye see your calling, brethren, how that not many wise men after the flesh, not many mighty, not many noble are called* (1Corinthians1: 26). You are where you are today, a minister's wife; not because you are better than others but by the grace of God (1 Corinthians 1:29, Ephesians 2:8-9). What a privilege!

Begin to see yourself and your husband's assignment from a positively different perspective from now on. What a joy, God chose you!

Exemplary Lifestyle

Your lifestyle, without any doubt speaks volumes! To be a minister's wife is to have been given as an example to your world, in essence (John 13: 15). Remember the saying: example is the best teacher? Certainly, people will read you. Whether you like it or not, they will do as you do. So, remember to:

> ***Let no man despise thy youth; but be thou an example of the believers, in word, in conversation, in charity, in spirit, in faith, in purity.***
>
> 1Timothy 4:12

Exemplary lifestyle is one major way to 'press'

successfully as a minister's wife.

Surprisingly, I have discovered that the public life of some minister's wives is radically different from their private lives. This ought not to be so. In public, some are 'angels', but are exact opposite in private. Do not be hypocritical! Reject self-deceit at all cost! You must learn to be consistent if you must make impact.

Your thoughts, words, walk, actions and behaviour should be such that boosts the work of the ministry. Labour to enter into that rest and refuse to fall after the same example of unbelief like some do (Hebrews 4: 11).

Your lifestyle – private and public, should not make people detest God or the ministry; rather, it should attract people and enhance the ministry. Let your life be an example for others to follow in your footsteps (I Peter 2: 21). For:

> ***Ye are our epistle written in our hearts, known and read of all men:***
>
> 2 Corinthians 3: 2

Like an epistle, people are reading you. The truth is that you have no 'secret' life to live! When I came to this understanding many years ago, I decided to sow my life as a seed in the most fertile soil of God's kingdom as a minister's wife, and I tell you: it is most rewarding!

Without gainsaying, it is overly important that you walk your talk and talk your walk! Many have and still are taking giant strides and leaving enviable footprints on earth today as minister's wives through exemplary lifestyle, come on and join the company; I can assure you – you will be glad you did!

FOOD FOR THOUGHT

"Whether you become a gold pot, Or a mud pot is not the maker's decision; but yours."

Kenneth Copeland

Chapter 2

It Begins With Understanding!

... Give me understanding, and I shall live.

Psalms 119:144(b)

One early morning, while working out on the treadmill, the Spirit of God began to speak to me clearly on the subject of understanding. He said to me several times: 'get understanding.'

As I began to meditate on this, it dawned on me that the word 'UNDERSTANDING' is actually made up of two separate words: 'under' and 'standing'. From these two words, we can deduce that: How well you 'stand' in life is determined largely by what is underneath you. In other words, what is 'under' determines how well you 'stand'.

What is actually under has a long way to go in determining how well you stand. Where I come from, there is a local saying that when you tell a lame man that the luggage on his head is bent, he would reply that the problem is not from the top! The bend is actually from under, (i.e. the bottom) not from the top. How true!

To put it in another way, if you must correct the crookedness of any luggage on the head, it must be from right under where the luggage is resting; because that is the base where the support, the reinforcement actually is. So, how well you 'stand' is a function of what is 'under' you.

As a pastor's wife, therefore, how well you function has a lot to do with what is under you; that is to say what you are standing upon.

As you are aware, in most cases what is 'under' is usually invisible. It is usually buried underneath the earth. So, we can actually refer to what is under as a foundation. Take buildings for example.

No matter how big, complex or comfortable a building is there is something it stands upon which albeit unseen is responsible for its strength and beauty. That thing is the foundation of the building; it lies under the gigantic structure and is responsible for making it stand! That is why it is a known fact whether you are a builder or not, that if there is a problem with the foundation of a building that building cannot stand the test of time.

So in essence, how well you stand, function and ultimately fulfill destiny as a minister's wife has a lot to do with your understanding. Understanding is it! That is the indispensable foundation upon which you can build a meaningful and impactful life.

Let's look at these two scriptures:

> ***Give me understanding, and I shall live***
>
> Psalms 119:144

> ***...and with all thy getting get understanding.***
>
> Proverbs 4:7

O that God will unfold to you a better understanding of who you are as a minister's wife and where to stand so that life can be progressively fulfilling! You cannot have a good understanding of this and not live an outstanding life.

What then, is 'understanding'? It means insight that goes beyond the surface or the obvious. It is knowledge that goes beyond the superficial to the very root of issues. According to Dr. David Oyedepo, 'Understanding makes outstanding.' So, for anything to be outstanding, understanding is a must. If understanding is so important, then what exactly do you need to understand as a minister's wife?

First, understand your multi-dimensional nature as

a minister's wife.

Secondly, understand your husband's ministry, how it affects you and how to position yourself for an undeniable, outstanding and effectual life and ministry.

Let us examine these two crucial areas where adequate understanding is required.

Your Multi-Dimensional Nature

First, let us look at your multi-dimensional nature from these four perspectives as:

A Woman

- God is your creator
- At salvation Jesus becomes your savior
- As you grow in him, He becomes your Lord indeed.

A Wife

- To your husband

I will discuss this in detail later in this book.

A Mother

- To your biological children
- To your spiritual children.

A Minister

- Ministry as you will soon discover, is much more

about service and impact than just title.

Each of these four will be discussed one after the other briefly here.

As a woman

God is your creator; Genesis 1:26-27. He created you in His own image and after His likeness. You originated from Him. Your root is in the Almighty God, what a privilege! He also put inside of you the seed of dominion! He created you whole, unique, complete and special. There was no deficiency in you when God your creator created you. You are fearfully and wonderfully made (Psalms 139:14).

So, as a woman, whatever your race, color, educational background etc, you are one of a kind and very special indeed. I am not just trying to make you feel good or excited; I am simply stating the truth as it is. God says concerning you in Jeremiah 13:3, *...I have loved you with an everlasting love.* Read also Isaiah.54: 10 & 43:4.

However, you must keep in mind the fact that God is the Creator of all – born again or not.

Then, when you got born again and consciously decided and gave your life to Jesus Christ, He became not only your creator, but also your Saviour. A personal relationship with Jesus Christ is established at this point in your life. This is the most important decision of your life. It is actually the beginning of a productive and fulfilling journey in life and especially as a minister's wife.

I gave my heart to Jesus and accepted Him as my savior many years ago as a teenager and I'm so glad I did; nothing compares to it, it has been getting sweeter by the day!

If I may ask: Do you have a personal relationship with Jesus as your savior? Do you have assurance of heaven? In case you don't, this is the best time to do so-right now! Until you do, you are only playing a game of religion and fooling yourself. This is not optional, it is mandatory. Or do you need to re-dedicate your life to Jesus Christ? Now is the best time to do so (2 Corinthians 6:2)! May you not live a life of vanity! Meditate on this scripture:

> ***Marvel not that I said unto thee, Ye must be born again.***
>
> John 3:7

Being a minister's wife is not a license to enter heaven, salvation which is a personal relationship with Jesus Christ is: I hope you know that. The earlier you understand this and apply yourself to it, the better for you.

Some minister's wives live and act in a manner that

make you wonder whether they have heaven in view as their future home. Do remember that it is salvation that gives you access to heaven and if you do not end your journey in heaven as a minister's wife you are of all men most miserable!

You need to treasure, protect and build on this relationship on a continuous basis; it is what guarantees you a place in eternity, and without it life is a complete waste! So, as a born again minister's wife, He is not only your creator, He is now also your Saviour.

Also, as you advance and progress in your walk with God and begin to yield your all to Him, surrendering to His leading at all times and in all areas of your life; He becomes your Lord. Please be aware that this is a process and it is not automatic; your conscious, deliberate, continuous and willing surrendered-ness to His will and word is required here. Self and its deeds must be mortified in you and Christ exalted, as a lifestyle. Like the scripture says:

He must increase, but I must decrease

John 3:30

This is a conscious decision you have to make, especially in the position that you are in right now as a minister's wife; Jesus should not just be your Savior, you need to make Him your Lord! That means your relationship with Him graduates to the level where whatever He tells you to do, is what you do, no matter what. No one else can make this decision for you, not even your minister husband!

If I may ask: have you ever consciously made Jesus Christ your Lord or is He just your savior? How surrendered are you to His word in your day-to-day life? How dedicated are you to Him? Do you see Him as a loving father or a task-master? Does His word and commandment suit or grieve you? (I John 5:3)

Precisely in the year 1976, before I got married, I consciously decided and made Jesus my Lord and it has been a most excited journey ever since. My husband (fiancé then), even wrote a paper titled 'Sailing Under Sealed Orders' which both of us had to sign; surrendering to the authority of Jesus Christ as Lord for a life time!

A copy of this has been included in this book for your edification (see a copy of this at the end of this book). And, in all, the journey has been most exciting, fulfilling and rewarding; to say the least!

If you have never consciously made this decision, this is the best time to do so. You need to make Him Lord over your life, your church, your ministry, your relationships, your finances, and over everything that has to do with you.

So, God is your creator. When you get born again He becomes your Saviour. Then, as you grow in your relationship with Him He becomes your Lord; depending on the level of your dedication to Him as an individual, to the exclusion of all others.

You need to have a good understanding of this fact because it will affect every aspect of your life and being, as a minister's wife. When you walk and live with this understanding, your effectiveness will be enhanced and life will be more fulfilling.

It will help you ensure that you establish and maintain a quality walk with God on a personal note, all by yourself; apart from what others around you are doing. No one else can do this for you; not even your 'anointed' minister husband!

So, you have a responsibility towards God through Jesus Christ; because He is your Creator, Saviour and Lord. See to it that you don't only establish a quality relationship and walk with God, but also ensure that it is maintained.

Please be aware: that a relationship existed yesterday does not mean it is still there (and vibrant too) today, just like some people who were your friends years ago may no longer be your friends today. May your walk with God not become a thing of the past, or a thing of history.

So, the primary dimension of your nature as a minister's wife is that, you are created whole and complete as a woman and the Bible says: *'In Him we are complete'*. This is the best platform for you to relate well with your husband as a helper, because in Christ you are complete and entire, wanting (lacking) nothing.

This takes me to the next level of your multi-dimensional nature as a minister's wife, which shall be examined here:

As a wife

You are the only wife of your husband. God gave you to him as a precious, valuable gift and the moment you were joined together in marriage the bible says you became one flesh! You need to ensure that you maintain a healthy husband/wife relationship as this will not happen automatically or simply because you are ministers of the gospel.

God's word declares:

> ***...for this cause shall a man leave father and mother, and shall cleave to his wife, and they two shall be one flesh.***
>
> Matthew 19:5

For the avoidance of doubt, to 'leave' in the above scripture implies gaining independence from, and being able to take steps without undue recourse to or influence from friends and family.

To 'cleave' means to be inseparably joined (glued) to someone without the existence of any interfering space in between them. This is marriage the bible way!

You must ensure that there is proper 'cleaving', otherwise loneliness will stare you right in the face while you remain helpless. Of course I am not implying that you should always follow him around or anything like that in the name of cleaving to your husband!

However, wherever possible and practicable, you should go with him; but bear in mind that this may not be possible all the time and should not be an impediment to your relationship. Cleaving in marriage is something that you have to cultivate consciously and on a continuous basis.

Two vital keys that will properly help you cleave to your minister husband in marriage are:

Trust: this means believing and expecting only the best from your minister spouse every time. It also means that you believe that your husband means well and that his intentions are pure. 1 Corinthians13: 7. I know this may sound a little 'strange': to always see only the good side of your husband and not give in to the temptation of yielding to suspicion sometimes!

To be sure, trust does not imply that your husband is always right, especially because your trust of him will be based on your experiences with him; but the bottom line of trust is that you commit him to God who alone can keep him and then choose to relate with him on the basis of confidence, trusting God to work out whatever might be out of place as you co-operate with him.

Communication: this means using words, actions, body language, letters etc with a view to making your husband not only listen to what you have to say, but for him to also understand what you are saying and feeling too. You must ensure that you also understand what he is saying and feeling per time as well.

Remember that as wife to him, it is God's injunction that you be a helpmeet (and to ensure that he is the same to you too). So, see to it that you are a contributor to his life in measurable and quantifiable terms! Be an addition and a plus to him and not a distraction, not a minus or a liability. This is the primary reason why God brought you in particular into his life.

One question I ask myself from time to time is *'What can I do today to add to my husband's life?'* Sometimes, I deliberately ask him what I can do to help or how I can make a difference in specific areas of his life. You can do the same thing, rather than assume that he is all right all by himself or that whatever help you render to him is on target. Make it a point of duty to occasionally ask him, 'what can I do for you?'

Then, on a personal note; ask yourself (between you and your God), what you can do as a plus to his life before the day runs out. Call on the Spirit of God inside you to guide you and give you insight into the innermost part of your husband's being so that you can perceive what his needs are and how you can help to make a difference. As you do that, the Spirit of God inside you will guide you; He will show you areas of attention and things to do.

These may appear insignificant-like: but perhaps a gentle neck or back massage at the end of a hard day's work, helping to charge his mobile phone at the right time, putting on the water heater to ensure no delay when he's ready to take his bath, putting off the television set so he could have a restful sleep when most needed, or even helping to wash and iron his briefs when he is too tired to do so himself.

All these little acts of kindness, especially when engaged in consistently, always make a huge difference in the long run. As you do, you will discover that you are not only meeting his needs but that you are also actually strengthening the husband/wife relationship between you. Plus: he won't be able to get you out of his mind even if you are out of his sight!

Refuse to validate in your life the general belief that men are the ones that should always reach out to women –giving and giving in every way possible, while the women should simply settle 'comfortably' into the role of collectors!

Proverbs 31:11(a) says that the heart of a virtuous woman's husband safely trusts her. That must be because she makes a difference in his life in every sphere.

Make it a point of duty to find something that you can do daily to add to your husband's life spiritually, emotionally, physically etc. Spiritually for instance, when was the last time you prayed for him? This is one major thing you must do for your minister husband on a daily basis if you expect him to flourish and see results in ministry. You know him better than any other person because you see him to the closet. So, you are in a better position to know what to pray for. Others pray for him, why can't you do the same thing? You will make it!

As a mother

In this third segment, the motherhood dimension

of your nature shall be examined. As a minister's wife; motherhood, as it relates to you: you must understand is not only to your biological children. It covers two main areas. It is about:

- Motherhood to your biological children
- Motherhood to your spiritual children

Now that you are a minister's wife, you are a mother; a spiritual nourisher of children, God's children (your biological children inclusive). This is a spiritual responsibility! Carry this consciousness everywhere you go and in your daily living. You may not look like it, and some of these spiritual 'children' may even be older than you, but that notwithstanding God has given you the unique privilege and responsibility of motherhood.

Nourish, groom, treat, handle, grow, and mother them the way you would have your biological children. You do not need to inform them or announce to them that you are their mother, or for that matter even require/compel them to call you 'mummy', 'mother' or whatever! Just carry yourself respectfully like one before them!

Remember: Mother the people, don't murder them! Mother them, carry them in your heart, love them, nurture them, reprove them, and draw them close. Just like a natural mother does, you need to feed them (spiritually and even physically where and when needed).

Also care for them, teach them, advise them, counsel them and discipline them in love, wisdom and in private; never be condescending or condemnatory in your approach. It is your duty as a mother to nurture them as you decorate, beautify and pray for them. Simply put: serve them (Matthew 23:11)!

What else should you do as a mother?

Live an exemplary lifestyle before your children (biological and spiritual). You be an example. Let your children see you living out the word of God on a daily basis, that way you will make a lasting positive impression on their lives like no preaching or lecturing can!

John Maxwell said: "Your character is your most effective means of persuasion"; and nowhere is this more applicable than in the lives of our children (biological and spiritual).

Don't live a life of double standards before them; you know, saying one thing and doing another. Be a woman of faith, virtue and transparent integrity.

Show gratitude. Whether it's your biological or spiritual children, express appreciation for everything they do, no matter how little or seemingly insignificant. This becomes more pertinent particularly when they do things, which are their "duty" or "responsibility", like doing chores, running errands for you or giving you gifts. Don't be 'lord' over them, expecting them to be at your beck and call all the time.

Learn to say 'thank you', 'I appreciate you', I'm grateful' and many more such to them. Don't take it for granted that they are available to serve you; show gratitude to them for whatever they contribute to your life, family or the work of the ministry.

Grow them spiritually. Invest into your children's lives spiritually by praying for them and teaching them the precepts of the Lord. For your biological children, this should be done right from an early age. Take time to give a listening ear to them so as not only to be able to know what's happening to them but also to be able to provide godly instruction and counsel. Remember not to make your discussions with them subject of any discussion with others; keep their confidences.

These life-transforming gems have radically affected my life and ministry positively, and still do; I know they will transform yours too if you diligently apply them!

As a minister

This is the fourth dimension of your nature as a minister's wife. The primary duty of a minister is to serve. So, ministry simply means service. That is why the bible talks about the work, service of the ministry **(Ephesians 4:12).** Ministry is all about service. So, if you are not serving then you are not in ministry.

Ministry is service, it is not about titles; it is about contribution, it is not about position. As earlier mentioned, it is about investment. Position can be very deceptive and many people do not realise that position without corresponding function is mockery!

Positions come and go, but when you function well in a particular office, the people whose lives you have impacted will never forget you, as you will remain in their memories all the days of their lives. With or without title and or position, the people that you have impacted live to remember and respect you because you were relevant to their lives

Please don't get me wrong, there is nothing scripturally wrong with titles or positions in ministry in themselves; as long as there are corresponding functions to match: but these should not be your focus or motivation in ministry, service and contribution should.

May I ask you, beloved co-labourer: where you are serving? As a minister's wife in the work of the ministry, whose lives are you impacting? I am not talking about what your husband is doing, neither am

I referring to church attendance! When you attend church service you are not serving God, which is why it is called 'church service,' because it is God who services you! I am talking about contribution to the cause of your father's kingdom.

Obviously, there are many areas in the house of the Lord where you can productively invest and develop your talent, gifts, training, resources and time to serve God. Be sure to find a place for quality service in your local assembly and be contribution-conscious in your outlook as a minister's wife.

Like me, your uttermost desire should be: that as stated in Matthew 25: 23, when you see your maker face to face at the end of your journey here on earth, to hear Him say to you: "well done, good and faithful SERVANT". Notice that is says 'servant', not 'minister's wife': but 'servant.' May you hear that from the Lord at the end of your journey here on earth!

Having discussed your multi-dimensional nature under four segments above, which is the first area where you require adequate understanding for you to be effective as a minister's wife; let us now examine the second area where you need adequate understanding to be effective.

His Ministry And How You Fit Into It

Before you can offer help and make a difference as you should, there is a need for you to have a hands-on, working knowledge and understanding of what your husband's calling and assignment are. You must know this like your very face!

The Bible says:

> ***...yea, if thou criest after knowledge and liftedst up thy voice for understanding; ... then shalt thou understand ...***
>
> Proverbs 2: 3, 5

Ask relevant questions about any 'grey' areas and make sure you fully understand what his assignment entails. This you may have to do regularly, as often as occasion demands. This is one of the secrets that help me personally as a minister's wife. Never assume that you understand what you don't, the consequences may be too much for you to bear!

Not only that, you should also accept your husband's assignment as yours too; and seek a good knowledge and understanding of it. Get to know, properly, what his calling is all about and what it entails. Remember:

> ***My people are destroyed for lack of knowledge ...***
>
> Hosea 4:6

Don't be an ignorant and uninformed minister's wife!

You see, if you must do your minister husband good and not be an impediment to his assignment, you must constantly seek to have a good working knowledge of his calling. Then and then alone will you be able to fully identify with his calling and then function properly as his helper in truth and indeed.

Worthy of note however, is the fact that: this is not a 'once –and- for- all' thing, because vision is progressive. As the days and years go by, keep abreast of latest instructions and directions from God concerning your husband's calling. This way, you will not only be up to date and current as far as his vision is concerned; but you will also be able to offer relevant help, counsel and support for every phase of the assignment. Also, you will be able to provide relevant prayer support for him and his assignment.

The Bible says:

> ***Good understanding procureth favour***
>
> Proverbs13: 15

Having a good understanding of his calling and plugging yourself into it will definitely bring you favour –with God, with your husband and with men generally. What a unique privilege indeed!

Generally speaking, the reason many women who are ministers' wives run into problems and confusion is because they do not have a good understanding of their husband's call. So, instead of working towards the same goal, they go in different directions and cause themselves and each other untold heartache and pain.

In some cases, many glorious ministries and callings have been stunted and lost on the platform of lack of understanding. I pray that yours will be different.

Another very important case for proper understanding of your husband's calling is that your call is embedded in his. God is not the author of confusion, if He chose you to be by your husband's side, then He has already endowed you with gifts and abilities that will beautifully complement his.

Your own God-given vision and goals in life cannot be at variance with your husband's, neither will it constitute a distraction to his work or be completely off tangent from his own God-given vision.

You are both meant to join forces together, pull in the same direction with hearts beating as one and feet going in the same direction; albeit through different routes! This is the beauty of understanding.

I cannot help but think that Eve probably did not quite understand and or identify fully with the task given to her husband, Adam. This caused her to make a negative impact in her husband's life, the consequences of which we are all too familiar with today.

Ensure that you handle your call with DISCRETION (i.e. the ability to make wise decisions by choosing from expedient and inexpedient options) and all faithfulness to Him that has called you. The high calling of God is an enviable position and you have no idea how many women wish they were in your shoes.

To be married to not just a believer, but also a minister of the gospel in whatever capacity is an awesome privilege. You need to know the heartache some are experiencing in their homes; maybe because they have unbelievers (non-Christians) as husbands or Christian husbands who are not willing to grow in the things of God. You are blessed! See yourself as such and conduct yourself accordingly.

The Importance Of Your Attitudes

It is pertinent to say here, that the success or failure of your husband as a minister has a lot to do with your attitude.

God's word says:

Every wise woman buildeth her house but the foolish

plucketh it down with her hands.

Proverbs 14:1

The building or the destruction of any 'house' (family, ministry) is dependent to a very large extent on the woman of the house. As a minister's wife, you should be a co-builder of the ministry with your husband, not one that pulls it down.

Your attitude as the minister's wife either builds or pulls down the work of the ministry. However, it is easier to pull down than to build and so the importance of your attitude cannot be over-emphasized.

Attitude can be defined as the way you think and act, how you see and interpret situations and circumstances around you.

As a minister's wife you must possess the right attitude towards your husband, your family, the ministry, the brethren and the church of Christ at large. Your position as a minister's wife sets you up, as an exemplary figure and many will watch your attitude; whether you realize it or not. There is therefore, a need to cultivate attitudes that enhance success, while at the same time doing away with attitudes that can be harmful.

Things like sulkiness, favoritisms, moodiness, anger, hatred, bitterness, depression, covetousness and the like must be done away with. Rather than attract, they repel. You are to be a source of joy to many, a life spring, a comfort to your husband, your home, to the brethren and people around you.

Please be aware: you are a helpmeet to your husband and not his boss, a source of encouragement not of discouragement, a companion not his competitor, an assistant or adviser not a director or dictator. See him as God's servant and treat him as you would a leader of God's people. Show that you believe in him and what God is doing in his life and through him. Do not be a thorn in his flesh or his life and ministry.

Also, your attitude to the brethren or people in general should be positive. You should not see your position as a minister's wife as an opportunity to harass, humiliate and 'deal' with those who have 'offended' you at one time or the other.

Resist every tendency for arrogance, pride and haughty spirit, but *'humble yourself under the mighty of God ...'* (1 Peter 5:6) because *'...before honor is humility'* (Proverbs 5: 33). As you humble yourself, God will make the grace required available for you to function effectively.

Your attitude to the work of the ministry, your involvement and contributions, no matter how small is also important and should be carefully looked into. Remember, you are an example. If your attitude shows that the work is not important to you or that you are undisciplined, this picture will register on those around you and before long they will also begin to do likewise, and the work of the ministry will be negatively affected. At all times, check your attitudes and make amends where and when necessary.

There are good attitudes like meekness, humility, compassion, and the like that bring you and those around you to success and there are terrible attitudes which can undo every success God has granted you and your husband in ministry. Embrace and imbibe the positive ones and reject the negative ones.

You cannot afford to have a wrong attitude.

Don't be title-crazy, because ministry is not about titles as I have already mentioned, but impact and affecting the lives of people positively for Christ. Don't misuse this opportunity; rather let God be glad that he made the right choice in calling you in particular. Remember ministry is 'work' not just mere title and your 'attitude' will determine your 'altitude' in life.

Understanding Your Position

Every position has its functions and responsibilities,

which must be properly understood if one must occupy the position well.

First, why do you need to understand your position as a minister's wife? You need to understand your position because:

Understanding your position will help you to know how to conduct yourself. Every position has its demands and until you fulfil the demands, you will not be able to function effectively. You need to know how to carry yourself, how to conduct yourself, what is expected of you, and what you should not be found doing.

I love what the bible says in this scripture:

> ***All things are lawful unto me, but all things are not expedient; all things are lawful for me, but I will not be brought under the power of any.***
>
> I Corinthians 6:12

You know the word 'expedient' means 'profitable'. All things are lawful but not all things are profitable. In other words, as a minister's wife, there are certain things that in themselves are not necessarily sinful but which an understanding of your position forbids you from getting involved in because they are not profitable and could detract from your office.

For example, some women can afford to dress in a suggestive manner, buy clothes or jewellery on credit, borrow clothes or money from others, go anywhere at any time, eat just about anywhere and generally conduct themselves in a less than appropriate manner. But you cannot afford to behave anywhere near these because there will be way too much at stake for you as a minister's wife. Others are looking up to you and you are meant to be an example for them to follow as an honourable minister's wife.

Be open and available without being seen as having favourites amongst the people that God has placed under your care. This is what understanding your position does for you.

Understanding your position will help you maintain order and sanctity. If you play your role well, your marriage and home will be the better for it because in an atmosphere of order your husband will be at his best at work and at home.

Rather than always hide under the cloak of being busy and avoid you, he will always look forward to coming home at the end of a hard day's work, because he knows he will come home to peace and order.

Thus: any temptation to have 'wandering eyes' will be easy for him to resist; thereby maintaining the sanctity of your marriage relationship. Your functioning in your position will bring sanctity and order to your home and then God's blessings will follow as well.

Your husband will be at his very best because you are a blessing and not a distraction, and you do not weigh him down with unnecessary demands or issues. By so doing, you are building, rather than plucking down. Proverbs 14:1. Your own home shall not be plucked down!

Understanding your position will facilitate your being your best. When you know how to conduct yourself as a minister's wife, you know what is expected of you and you conduct yourself accordingly, your best begins to come out. Self reduces as God increases in your life.

Personally, there are certain things God has enabled me to be able to do over the years which I never dreamt I would be able to do, like speaking before large crowds of people. The mere thought of it alone would have sent my heart racing in fear. But today to the glory of God, even though I am still very far from being an expert at it, God has helped me to gain amazing confidence at public speaking as I have yielded myself to him and given myself unreservedly to the demands of my position as a ministers' wife. That's how it works!

There are certain things that you also may have thought you would never be able to do or overcome, but trust me; by virtue of the discipline that your position subjects you to, you will soon discover that what you thought was impossible is very possible with you.

You will get better and sharper as latent abilities that you never even knew you possessed begin to surface in your life. Then you will become a great asset to your husband's ministry as well as a blessing to people around you.

Now let's look at your functions in detail.

Functions Of A Minister's Wife

A vision supporter

Having fully understood your husband's vision and calling, you are supposed to provide invaluable support to him and his assignment. You are not the visionary; you did not deliver his vision to him, so your job is not to direct, instruct or tell him how to run a vision that was not given to you directly. You are a vision supporter so don't attempt in any way not even in your heart, to usurp authority over your husband the visionary.

I never cease to be amazed at ministers' wives who 'struggle' for the microphones with their husbands! Some even think they can do a better job of preaching than their husbands or that they are more 'current' with God and therefore should lead the way while their husbands follow! Two people cannot hold one microphone at the same time because there will be confusion.

Please, be aware that: beside every successful man is a successful woman. Mind you I said 'Beside', not 'Ahead of' or 'Behind. So, rather than struggling to usurp authority over him or competing with him for that matter, why don't you look at the areas of his life that require attention and ask God to wisely show you what to do to help him out?

My dear friend, how well are you supporting your husband and his God-given vision? Are you a vision supporter indeed or a vision detractor? It will be wise of you to begin to consider action steps that you need to take right now in order to be more functional as a vision-supporter?

A husband caretaker

He is your husband and you have the privilege of God to care for him. Find out areas where you can meet his needs, believe God for wisdom to be able to identify how you can care for him because if you don't care for him, be sure that someone else will; and by the time you realise it, it may be too late.

The reason many anointed men of God fall on the laps of other women is because they have wives who are not caring. You need to remember that your anointed husband is human; he is an earthen vessel who is subject to like feelings and desires as other men (remember Samson). Thus do your best to take care of him.

Be genuinely concerned about his well-being and see to it that no one takes your place in his life. This is not to say that you should be suspicious of every woman who comes around your husband; no, but be sensitive and do your part leaving nothing to chance.

Somebody once said that men are simply boys in trousers. No matter how anointed your minister husband is, don't ever think he is a superman. Even Jesus was tempted by the devil, but Jesus overcame; and so will your husband.

So, make sure you mother him with care; ensuring that you see to his being comfortable at all times. Don't hinder the flow of the anointing of God upon his life. Be sensitive to his needs. Just like you, he has spiritual, physical and emotional needs. Be sensitive to them all.

Talking about his needs spiritually, you know he's into a spiritual assignment. How are you mothering him in that respect? You should be able to find a place of contribution. You know he has an engagement for instance, maybe to speak in the church or to perform some other functions by virtue of his position in one arm of the ministry or another, don't just take things for granted. Make time out to pray for him, take him to God in prayer; come against every plan of the enemy concerning his life.

As a minister's wife, if you cannot pray for your husband, whom do you expect to pray for him? Even if others are praying for him, they are just helpers. You are the one to take this as a primary assignment.

When was the last time you prayed for your husband? If your husband's success depended on your prayer contribution, how successful will he be?

He has physical, emotional and mental needs too. Depend on the grace of God to enable you be there for him when he needs you most. For instance, when he needs to eat don't pretend that he is too anointed to need food! Don't deny him sex in the name of spirituality! (These issues will be addressed in greater details later in this book).

A follower and humble monitor

You should follow him as he follows Christ and charts the course in the pursuit of the vision that God has committed into his hands. Maybe he's over a church somewhere; as the pastor's wife, it is part of your followership to attend church services (and punctually too) irrespective of whether you are working full time in the ministry or you are involved in some other job or vocation.

Absenteeism or late coming to ministry functions is unbecoming of your position as a minister's wife, except where it is absolutely unavoidable and in which case God himself understands.

Isn't it a shame that sometimes, other people like church members, members of staff etc, are more committed to the work of the ministry than some ministers' wives? Some of these people give their lives to God's assignment as if that's the only thing they do. Take a cue from that and follow your husband's assignment doggedly.

God has blessed women with an unusual ability to sense and perceive things much quicker than men; women are very intuitive. Most times, men are very busy focussing on the big picture as they tend to be goal getters.

Be a faithful follower by drawing your husband's attention to some issues that you perceive are worth bringing to his notice which he may not even be aware of. (Of course not petty issues that do not affect the work in any way or that will only distract or make him unnecessarily upset).

Be all eyes to see what areas require attention and improvement with wisdom: At the appropriate time bring them to his notice with the attitude of a helper/ humble monitor, not a "know-it-all" instructor!

Make sure however that you don't feed your husband with information that will dampen his spirit or negatively affect the anointing. Don't discuss with him issues that can make him begin to harbour hatred or bitterness towards others. This will not be appropriate, and at the end of the day it will bounce back to you.

Remember that he who digs a pit shall fall into it (Ecclesiastes 10:18). Engaging in discussions that could engender anger, make him become suspicious of certain people or detest the presence or contributions of some people in the assembly is not proper.

Constantly believe God for wisdom in your communications with him, and ensure that your motive is right; because God sees and judges your motives. So, possess a right motive and pure intention as a humble follower and contributor. Even if the situation is dire, handle it with great care; take the poison out of it first and don't influence your husband's perspective with your own biased stance!

A role model

As I mentioned briefly earlier on, you are meant to be

a role model beginning from your 'Jerusalem', which is your home. Be a role model to your family members, your children and to the people you are privileged to come in contact with.

You should however never make a mistake to get swollen-headed especially when people commend you and your impact upon their lives, because the largest room in the world is the room for improvement. There is always a better way of doing whatever you do in life. Where you are and what you are doing right now is good; thank God for your life, but there is a place called 'there', a place of excellence! We are all journeying towards it and by the grace of God, we together shall get there.

A role model is one who charts a course. A role model is one who sets a pace. A role model is one who sets a worthy example to follow. What you do, your children will unconsciously begin to do. If you speak abusive words, your children will do the same thing. If you tell lies, you can't stop them from doing so. If your room and home is usually messy and unkempt, know that they will follow your footsteps. May you be found as a worthy role model in Jesus' name.

In order to be able to carry out the above functions effectively, you require:

Discipline. Discipline means self-control; it also

means restraint. And you know, self-discipline is the best kind of discipline. The control and restraint under which you put yourself, not the one under which someone else puts you. Begin to cultivate that today and see how fulfilling it will be to function in your God-given role as a minister's wife.

Wisdom. Wisdom is very crucial to your effectiveness as a minister's wife. Foolishness destroys faster than wisdom builds. One prayer, I believe I have prayed the most in my life and which I still pray is the prayer for wisdom. This is because the Bible says it is the principal thing. You can't have too much of wisdom.

Wisdom means correct application of knowledge, knowing what to do to get your desired result and doing it; and the way to get it is through the word of God. This explains why the Bible says:

> ***Thou, through thy commandments, hast made me wiser than mine enemies.***
>
> Psalms 119:98

To acquire more wisdom therefore, you need more of God's word.

Meekness. This means humility. Pride must die so that God can be exalted, for God resists the proud but gives grace only unto the humble. James 4: 6. You must understand that pride is very subtle and deceptive.

This, among other things is because it begins from the heart, and before you know it, it starts to find expression in every area of your life.

What is the state of your heart right now? Sure enough, you don't need any 'prophet' to tell you whether you are proud or not; you know yourself better than anyone else and your heart bears you witness. The earlier you get rid of that pride the better for you and the more effective you become.

Haven gone through the areas where you require adequate understanding so you can be effective, now receive the grace to be obedient to the instructions of the Lord as it concerns fulfilling your role as a minister's wife, in Jesus great name, amen.

FOOD FOR THOUGHT

"You cannot find until you define"

John Mason

Chapter 3

Accept Your Peculiarity

As a minister's wife, you are peculiar - very special, unusual, important, positively strange, uniquely favored by God. You occupy a very unique position. This informs why concerning you, the scripture says:

> ***But ye are a chosen generation, a royal priesthood, an holy nation, a peculiar people; that ye should shew forth the PRAISES of him who hath called you out of darkness into His marvellous light, which in time past were not a people, but are now the people of God: which had not obtained mercy but now have obtained mercy***
>
> 1 Peter 2:9

In the above scriptures, the phrase: 'Ye are' indicates that presently, right now, this is who you are, not who you will become. As a minister's wife, believer in Christ Jesus, you are a chosen generation, a royal priesthood, an holy nation and a peculiar people.

With all these qualities, you simply stand out; and you cannot but draw the attention of people. You are a special and rare species of person on earth. Isn't it wonderful to know that all these adjectives qualify who you are? Let's take a closer look at these 'identification marks'.

A Chosen Generation

You – yes, you are a generation. This is because the things that you do or do not do outlive you. Long after you are gone, your actions and inactions will keep reverberating through the ages. When you get born again however, you become a 'chosen generation.'

At salvation, you responded to God's choice upon your life. God chose you to be His very own child under His own family roof. You did not merit this, neither were you the one that chose Him; rather, He chose you. This is an immense privilege that should not be taken for granted.

We read this outstanding statement about our relationship with God: *"We loved him because he first loved us.* (1John 4:19). Again *"...for he is Lord of lords, and King of kings: and they that are with Him are called, and CHOSEN, and faithful"* (Revelations 17:14) because: *"God hath chosen the foolish things of the world to confound the wise; and God hath chosen the weak things of the world to confound the things which are mighty;"* (1Corinthians 1:27).

The Cambridge Advanced Dictionary defines the word 'chosen' as: "a small group of people who are treated better than other people, often when they do not deserve it". Amazingly, this is the group to which you belong!

To 'choose' means to decide what you want from a range of things or possibilities. So, God decided and picked you out of a range of possibilities. This means that there were and still are others that God could have picked, but He decided on you. What an election of grace! An understanding of this should help you conduct yourself in a most acceptable manner to God and impactful manner to men.

My husband, Bishop David Oyedepo often refers to an experience he had with God when he was being called into full time ministry. According to him, God told him that his call into the work of the ministry was a privilege and should not be handled lightly. He said God also told him that there are better hundreds and should he mess up with the assignment, it would be given to a 'better neighbor' of his. This informs and has affected his radical approach to ministry work in no small measure.

So, please be aware that you have been chosen by God as a minister's wife from a range of possibilities; not on the grounds of merit but mercy. Oh, I am eternally grateful to God for this choice of me! How about you? You must therefore ensure that God does not regret ever choosing you to be special before Him amongst all people upon the earth.

You are not just a minister's wife by chance or accident; but because God chose you. May be you would not have chosen to marry a minister if you 'had your way'. All the same, God found you, because you are chosen. It is one thing however, to be chosen by God but another for God not to regret choosing you.

Remember Saul in the Old Testament (1 Samuel 15: 11,26) and Judas in the New Testament (Acts 1:17,20-22). God's choice has sounded upon your life, you are privileged; handle that choice jealously. May God not regret over your life.

A Royal Priesthood

You are a royal priesthood. Not just an ordinary priesthood, but a royal one. So, as a minister's wife, you belong to royalty! Royalty is an indication that you are from the family of kings and queens due to the kingship of your Father (GOD). It also indicates that you are from the reigning class. Wherever you are, people must pay attention to you.

Like it was shown earlier from the scriptures: the Lord Jesus our mentor is *"Lord of lords and King of kings..."* (Revelations17: 14). Also, He is *"the first born of every creature.* Colossians 1: 15 makes us see our lineage clearly because we as believers are *"...his offspring..."* (Acts 17:28)

As a kingly priest and lord how should you conduct yourself? An earthly king conducts himself with all dignity because his subjects look up to him as an example for them to follow. So, you also must be aware that you are set up as an example to be emulated both as a believer and as a minister's wife. Therefore, you should conduct yourself graciously, with dignity and in an exemplary manner.

It is natural for people, especially those you are privileged by God to lead to imitate you in many areas of life. They may for instance consciously or unconsciously, talk, act, dress, eat and react like you do. You must therefore be a worthy example.

People learn much more by example than through any other means. If earthly kings are conscious of the fact that they cannot think, talk or walk anyhow, how much more should you; a minister's wife, a royal priesthood!

Watch your thoughts (Proverbs 23:7; 24:9; Ephesians 4:23), talk (Ephesians 4: 29; Ephesians 5:4; Proverbs 29: 11) and walk (Ephesians 5: 2, 5-8; 11). As a priest, you are of the lineage of the High Priest who is our Lord Jesus.

Thus, the law and the knowledge of our Lord should always be at hand so that you can teach and direct those that come your way, *"for the priest's lips should keep knowledge, and they should seek the Law at his mouth: for he is the messenger of the Lord of hosts"* (Malachi 2:7). Purify your thoughts, speak only gracious words and act the word of God always.

"The throne is established by righteousness" (Proverbs 16:12). So, as a royal priest you must conduct yourself according to righteousness. Righteousness must be your watchword in thought, word and deed.

Every king has a staff of office, which signifies authority. For the believer the rod (staff of office) is the word of God; *"...a rod out of the stem of Jesse ..."* (Isaiah 11:1), our Lord Jesus Christ himself. He is also known as *"...THE WORD of GOD..."* (Revelations 19: 13).

Therefore, the written word of God, the scriptures must constantly be in place in your heart and life. Never be lazy at the word. Let the word dwell in you richly, and in abundance (Colossians 3: 16). Make it your daily companion. This way, you can secure the Lord Jesus' presence with you and your rod of authority or staff of office will be in place.

A Holy Nation

The Lord said concerning you: *be ye holy: for I am holy". Peter 1:16. And again: "...holiness becometh thine house, O Lord, for ever.* Psalms 93:5.

As a minister's wife, you must live a holy life. This is not optional, it is mandatory. The old nature of sin has been replaced with that of the nature of God Himself, which is holiness.

Let your life – in thoughts, words and actions be an embodiment of holiness. In your **thoughts**, learn to think pure. There are things to think upon and there are others that you should not allow in your thoughts. (Philippians 4: 8). You must learn to tame, sanitize, purify and cleanse your thoughts. This will not happen on it's own; you have to take practical steps to get it done.

In your **words,** the scriptures command:

> ***Let no corrupt communication proceed out of your mouth, but that which is good to the use of edifying, that it may minister grace unto the hearers.***
>
> Ephesians 4: 29

You have a responsibility to watch your words, otherwise, your destiny may be washed out! Be careful about what you say. Don't just speak anyhow; learn to choose your words. Filthiness, foolish talking, jesting, which are not convenient should not be engaged in by you. (Ephesians 5: 4).

One secret I have found to be very helpful in this regard, personally is to think before you speak. Many people only think after they have spoken, so they keep regretting what they said; this ought not to be. The bottom line is: weigh your words before you speak them.

Holy living should also be demonstrated in your **actions**. God weighs actions (1 Samuel 2: 3). Discipline your disposition! The word of God commands: *And have no fellowship with the unfruitful works of darkness, but rather reprove them*. Ephesians 5: 11.

Demonstrate and practice holiness in your day-to-day living. This is a deliberate choice that you have to make as a result of your peculiarity, if you desire to be effective as a minister's wife.

You cannot afford to live in covetousness, lies, pride, hatred, bitterness, gossip, back-biting, malice, adultery, immorality, and the like any longer because God has called you to holy living!

Sin is a destroyer of destiny! It stings, stinks and

sinks people! You will not be a victim. Many ministries have been ruined because of the unholy life of ministers' wives.

Watch it and stop that sin before it stops you. That bitterness and malice with church members must end! Be reminded: *For sin shall not have dominion over you:* ... Romans 6: 14. You will make it!

A Peculiar People

According to the *Standard Dictionary of English Language* by Funk and Wagnall's, **"peculiar"** means: having a character exclusively its own, unlike anything else or anything of the same class or kind; to be special, separate, distinguished. It also means: something or someone which "belongs particularly or exclusively to someone, any private possession, extraordinary, queer, and rare.

With all these adjectives, you can see what God has made of you. A person though can be negatively peculiar, exhibiting wrong traits. But thanks be unto God who has made us positively peculiar with the ability to exhibit graceful qualities towards Him and towards our fellowmen.

In this context, God sees you as his very own peculiar, precious, special, treasure. "*...ye shall be a peculiar* *treasure unto me above all people; for all the earth is mine: ..."* (Exodus 19:5). So, you are peculiar to Him, just like a woman will treasure and guard her gold jewellery much more than all others.

You are so peculiar that just like there is no other person with your set of fingerprints on earth; there is no other woman like you in the sight of God. There may be some who are similar but none is exactly like you. There is no one else under the sun, (even if the person bears the same name with you, looks like you, has your features and qualities) like you.

Besides, there is a special plan and purpose of God for your life that is peculiar to you and no one else can fulfill it like you. Woman, stop comparing yourself with others. Regarding this, the Bible says:

> ***...but they measuring themselves by themselves, and comparing themselves among themselves, are not wise.***
>
> 11 Corinthians 10:12

Don't ever wish you were created a man. Never wish you did not marry a gospel minister. You are the best of you God could have created. Don't ever give room to discouragement even if you are laughed at, looked down upon, gossiped about or ignored.

Be moderate and decent such that your physical

appearance invites the respect of others rather than their scorn and shocking stares. Never walk according to worldly standards because you are from above. May the Lord help you to maintain a healthy balance.

Your relationship as a minister's wife to your husband can be likened to Christ's relationship with the Father. He said, "I and the Father are one..." (John 10:30), and according to His word in Ephesians 5: 31, you and your husband are one. Also, concerning Christ's relationship to the church: There is "...one body..." (Ephesians 4:4) and the "husband is the head of the wife, even as Christ is the head of the church ..." Ephesians 5: 23).

As a minister's wife, you are to minister primarily to your husband. Minister to his needs; both as a wife to a husband and as a minister to the servant of the Lord. This may entail duties, services and responsibilities; which only you as a wife can fulfill and which make you peculiar to him, amongst all others.

Look at the following examples of relationships very closely and you will see other areas where you may need to function and cause your peculiarity to be more pronounced in your relationship to God's servant, your husband.

Joshua's relationship with and servant-attitude

towards Moses (Exodus 33: 11): He stayed close to the mountain when all the others were in their tents. It is not surprising that he became Moses' successor.

Aaron and Hur's relationship with Moses during the battle (Exodus 17:12): They both stayed glued to Moses' side, refusing any form of distraction and maintained focus for as long as it was necessary to stay Moses' hands up. By their cooperation, Israel discomfited and prevailed over their enemies.

Elisha's faithfulness to Elijah (2kings 2): Even when all the other sons of the prophet chose to stay back knowing that Elijah was going to be taken away, Elisha followed unto the very end, not wishing to leave his master for any reason. Sure enough, he received a double portion of his spirit.

David's relationship as Saul's amour bearer (1 Samuel 16:21): In spite of the ill treatment and hatred of Saul, David served him faithfully. At the end of the day, he ascended the throne and became a man after God's own heart.

Ruth's relationship with Naomi, her mother – in – law (Ruth 1:16): This was dedication per excellence. Even when it seemed there was nothing to hang around Naomi for, Ruth stayed with her to her own discomfort. As expected, she was mightily rewarded and today has her name in the lineage of Jesus Christ.

John's affection to be a part of all that Jesus did is another example worthy of note (John 13: 23).

As a wife of God's servant, your closeness to him as the oracle of God Almighty is unique. In the above examples, each of them had to resist being attached to the crowd in order to faithfully wait upon God's servant. Their faithfulness was duly rewarded by God, for there is no service in the kingdom that is lost.

As a minister's wife you are peculiar and occupy a peculiar position in your husband's life and ministry. Make the most of this rare privilege and don't take it for granted.

For instance, you see him every day; both on the pulpit during ministrations and privately at home, right to his closet. You see Him as the servant of God with the unction of the Holy Spirit on him and also as a man of like passions in his natural estate.

At times of vulnerability there is a tendency to wonder what is so special about him and to be tempted to wait on him only as a wife would a husband and not as God's servant. As a wife, you should never despise the unction of God upon your husband and treat him only as a husband. He should also be treated as God's servant.

Waiting on your minister husband as God's servant and at the same time as a husband brings about a unique blending of services, which gives you a peculiarity. Each has its place and is most necessary to properly stand in your calling as a minister's wife. You must know when and how to relate with him as a husband as well as when and how to relate with him as a minister.

My dear husband, Bishop David Oyedepo is not just a husband to me; he is also my pastor. Only me can be both to him and vice versa. This I have always said both in private and in public. I am blessed, to say the least. It is a unique privilege of my life to be married to my pastor!

Benefits Of Your Peculiar Status.

The servant of God (your husband) can be likened to a spiritual fountain through which the living waters from heaven flows to quench the thirst of the thirsty. You as a minister's wife due to proximity can drink from his fountain anytime.

For example, as a result of the closeness between Jesus and his disciples, Jesus was able to tell them: "Unto you it is given to know the mystery of the kingdom of God: ..." (Mark 4:11). As his 'bride' and closest confidants they were always first partakers of the mysteries of the kingdom. **Revelation knowledge by the unction of God on your minister-husband's** life becomes easily accessible to you.

While others look forward to being ministered to, struggle, book appointment, observe necessary protocols, pray and believe God to be able to see him; you as his wife receive first hand ministrations without effort! Again you have the privilege and opportunity to be the first partaker of everything God is doing in his life and ministry.

There is also the opportunity to come in **contact with many other great men and women of God**, various ministers in the various ministry offices and locations and so the possibility to see the various moves of God in other ministries and ministers' lives; partake of their diverse unction and be in the forefront of God's move in the body of Christ. This is a very special privilege!

Then, there is **a greater opportunity to enjoy a harmonious family life compared to others**. Though this greatly depends on the depth of knowledge about marriage that both of you possess and practice, but there is still an added advantage over the marriages of most other people.

The knowledge of what God has said concerning marriage which both of you walks in gives you, the wife some sense of security over what other homes experience that lead to issues such as heartbreak, misunderstanding, chaos, divorce etc.

Please note that this does not imply that challenges will not come, they sure will. However, as ministers armed with the word of truth, such challenges become stepping stones; you scale through them and secure peace in your home. Mind you, not all ministers enjoy a fulfilled family life; but those who take heed to God's word on the subject of marriage do.

Also, as a minister's wife, though at times you may have to withdraw from the crowd; there are other times however that your attention will be needed. In such situations, the potential in you, which may never have come out, will begin to surface.

While others may live a life of non-service and lack of productivity, there are many challenges that will **stir up hidden potentials and creative characters in you**, which may never have been awakened if you were not married to a minister of the gospel. You as a minister's wife will have such unique opportunities and much more: to influence, impact and even mould other peoples' lives by the Spirit of God to His glory; thereby fulfilling destiny in ground style!

With a good understanding of all the above, it becomes easy to accept your peculiarity with joy, gratitude and every sense of mission. Even though as earlier said, you may sometimes need to withdraw from the crowd to enable you draw near to God and give yourself wholeheartedly to seeking God and exploring the companionship of the Holy Spirit.

So woman, accept your peculiarity; this will greatly enhance your performance and you will in turn begin to enjoy the above listed benefits and even much more.

It is important to note however that drinking of the unction of God upon your minister-husband's life is not automatic, despite the fact that you have the unique privilege of proximity peculiar to only you. It is required that you correctly position yourself for it.

Just like sitting at the bank of a river does not necessarily and automatically free you from thirst, that you are his wife does not give you automatic access to enjoying these benefits without rendering any service to him. You will have to earn it by working for it. That's why I mentioned earlier that your relationship to him is twofold: Relating to him as a wife and relating to him as a servant waiting upon the Lord's minister.

When you relate to him in the two ways discussed

above, you correctly position yourself for and earn your peculiarity. These two cannot be separated, if you want to experience and enjoy the benefits enumerated earlier on.

Remember, Michal despised David; her husband and king of Israel, when he danced before the Lord 'crazily.' As a result, instead of being blessed like others, she was cursed regardless of whether she was David's wife or not; because she refused to respect the unction of God upon her husband, the servant of God (2 Samuel 6: 14-23).

At a time when she ought to have related to David as a minister of God, she related to him as a husband and she paid for it dearly. May God grant you the wisdom to know how to relate with your minister husband correctly at all times and in all situations. You are in every way peculiar as a minister's wife both to your husband's family and ministry at large.

Accept your peculiarity! Don't hide it. Don't feel left out or inadequate. It is the power of God (Romans 1: 16) unto the fulfillment of all that salvation has to offer you as a minister's wife.

As you rejoice with God's choice of and for you, great joy becomes your portion and great results shall continue to spring forth from you. May the Lord open the eyes of your understanding to further see and appropriate your peculiarity in Him as a minister's wife, in Jesus name!

FOOD FOR THOUGHT

"Difficulties seldom defeat people; lack of faith in themselves usually does it."

John C Maxwell

Chapter 4

Run The Race Before You

Wherefore, seeing we also are compassed about with so great a cloud of witnesses let us lay aside every weight, and the sin which doth so easily beset us and LET US RUN with patience THE RACE THAT IS SET BEFORE US.

Hebrews12: 1

In the previous chapter we discovered that you are "a **chosen** generation, a **royal** priesthood, an **holy** nation, a **peculiar** people; that ye should show forth the praises of Him who hath **called** you out of darkness into his marvelous light." (1 Peter 2:9)

You have been chosen out of the multitudes to serve Christ and to also serve as a minister's wife. You have been called to a glorious destiny in Christ. Not because you are better than others, not on the grounds of merit but by the mercies of the Lord. You did not qualify for it, yet He decided to choose you to be the wife of a minister.

It Is A Race!

You must understand that being a minister's wife is a race in itself. The above scripture in Hebrews 12: 1 makes that very clear. God has set a race for you to run here on earth.

A race is a course, direction or path of life to follow. It is a race, not a title to carry or a position to occupy. The race is meant to be run by you. No one else can run the race on your behalf. You must accept responsibility and have a race mentality towards your position as a minister's wife.

An understanding of the fact that your being a minister's wife is a race will help you guide your affairs in life with discretion. Your perspective of life determines your interests. When you understand it as a race, it will positively affect your approach to it.

Naturally, everyone in a race focuses his eyes on the goal or target and adapts himself to the rules and regulations of it. He adapts to the discipline required, just because he has a target. So also, being a minister's wife is a race; you must have your eyes focused on the target and adapt yourself to the discipline, rules and regulations.

I believe this is why the Bible says:

The light of the body is the eye: if therefore thine

eye be single, thy whole body shall be full of light.
Matthew 6: 22

Let your eyes be single, focus on the target, refuse to be distracted or entangled, as you run this race. You will make it in Jesus name.

It Is Set Before You By God

It is very important to know that being a minister's wife is a race or course set before you by God Himself. Please be aware that I am not referring to self-appointed ministers. No, I am referring to ministers who have been genuinely called by God. You did not get married to your minister-husband by chance; not at all. It is in the plan and purpose of God for your life to be a minister's wife as discussed earlier on.

This appointment is not from man but from God Himself, for "...no man taketh this honour unto himself, but he that is called of God..." (Hebrews 5:4). It is a race that God Himself has set before you to run. An understanding of this truth will help you seek to please God, the one who has set this race before you, and not man. Do not seek to please man, but God.

Many people in ministry pre-occupy themselves primarily with how to render eye service or please men. Never be deceived into joining such people. Do not be 'face-full', but faithful.

To be faithful in a race means to keep your eyes on the track, the goal; and to keep running with all the strength you can muster. It means fixing your gaze, your total attention, on what God has called you to be and to do; refusing every form of distraction and applying all diligence to see to its execution (Isaiah 50:7).

On the other hand, to be 'face-full' means to engage in eye-service; to become men-pleasers and not God-pleasers. If you are not faithful as a minister's wife, God cannot commit more into your hands. This explains why the scripture says:

> ***He that is faithful in that which is least is faithful also in much: and he that is unjust in the least is unjust also in much.***
>
> Luke16: 10

People whom God place in positions of authority are usually those who have previously served faithfully in one capacity or another under someone else. Even if your husband who is a minister is working under a ministry, you should seek to please God first and then you will be able to please him whom God has put over you as the head in that ministry or organization.

Faithfulness is not optional, it is mandatory; it is a must for you as a ministers' wife. Faithfulness: primarily to God and then to man, in all areas of life; including ministry, family etc. This is non-negotiable.

This is why the Bible says concerning you in 1Timothy 3:11, that wives should be *"...faithful in all things..."*

How faithful have you been as a minister's wife in running this race set before you by God? Answer that question truthfully and begin to make amends today where necessary.

Run To Receive The Prize

Running the race God sets before you successfully qualify you to obtaining the prize. God is a God of purpose. He does not do things without a purpose; if He says for you to run this race, there is a reason for that, according to the scripture, it is because there is a prize to obtain. The bible says:

> ***Know ye not that they which run in a race run all, but one receiveth THE PRIZE? So run, that ye MAY OBTAIN.***
>
> 1 Corinthians 9:24

God, who has shown Himself to be "... a rewarder of those who diligently seek Him (and His will)" (Hebrews 11:6), has ordained that you obtain the prize; the reward for diligence in the area where He has called you.

However, you must understand that receiving the prize is not automatic. Even in the natural, not all that run in a race receive the prize. You must run according to the rules and with a determination to receive the prize. Running without receiving the prize is a waste of life, time and energy. As you are aware, it brings shame.

Saul in the Old Testament was called, chosen and anointed as king over Israel; but did not run the race to receive the prize. This was due to his disobedience to the word of God (1 Samuel 15:26-28). So, it is not enough to start the race; you must run it to the end, according to the rules before you can receive the prize.

Judas is a typical example in the New Testament, to teach us that if you do not take heed to yourself and to the word of God; it is possible to fall short of the plan of God for your life (Acts 1:16-17, 25), even in these last days.

You will not fail of the grace of God!

There are positive examples in scriptures of those who took heed and were diligent to run the race set before them, and thereby made full proof of their ministries and callings.

Joseph is a notable Old Testament example who suffered much wrong done against him, yet he was able to successfully go through and run his race to the end. To his brothers who tormented him, he said:

> ***Now therefore be not grieved, nor angry with yourselves, that ye sold me hither: for God did send me before you to preserve life.***
>
> Genesis 45: 5

Are you going through any difficulty or challenge as a minister's wife right now? Don't give up! Remember that quitters never win and winner never quit. Take courage! You can still run the race that God has set before you like Joseph did, and you will definitely receive the prize! Refuse to quit.

Mary, the mother of the Lord Jesus is also another notable example of someone who was called and who ran the race God set before her to the end faithfully - to be the mother and custodian of the saviour. There is no evil tied to her record, she had a clean and clear testimony. She was faithful from the time of receiving the call in Luke1: 28-38, till the bringing forth of the Lord and his death and resurrection.

The Bible records of her:

> ***Now there stood by the cross of Jesus his mother...***
>
> John19:25

And again, the scriptures say:

> ***... these all continued with one accord in prayer***

> ***supplications with women , and Mary the mother of Jesus..***
>
> Acts 1:14

Whatever can make you fail to obtain the prize as you run the race God has set before you as a minister's wife must be done away with! These include but are not limited to things such as distractions, discouragements, lusts etc. You must be determined to run in order to obtain.

If you do not succeed as a minister's wife, then you have frustrated God's grace. Remember:

> ***...every man that striveth for the mastery is temperate in all things...***
>
> 1 Corinthians 9: 25

To be temperate means to be able to exercise control, to be disciplined. So, discipline must be your watchword as a minister's wife if winning the prize is your goal.

By now, I am sure you must be wondering what kind of prize it is that is to be received. Interestingly, it is neither fame, nor money, nor possessions (although these may be part of the additions from God to you eventually).

But, for you to be able to hear the one who set the race before you say to you at the end of your journey: "*...well done, thou good and faithful servant: enter thou* *into the joy of thy Lord."* Matthew 25: 21; and for generations after you to remember you for good and call you "blessed," that is the ultimate reward. May this be your testimony at the end of the day! This is what I am personally looking forward to.

Cloud Of Witnesses

> ***Wherefore seeing we also are compassed about with so great a cloud of witnesses...***
>
> Hebrews 12: 1

The above scripture says: "seeing". This in essence is asking you to be aware (conscious) of this fact. You must be conscious of, know and see the great cloud of witnesses that compass you about as you run the race that God has set before you.

As a minister's wife, your domain of operation, your base is Zion, and the Bible says in Zion is:

> ***...an innumerable company of angels, the general assembly and the church of the first born which are written in heaven, God the judge of all, the spirits of just men made perfect, Jesus the mediator of the new Covenant, and the blood of sprinkling...***
>
> Hebrews12:22-24

What a roll call of witnesses!

In essence, all of heaven is at alert, watching you as

you run the race set before you; you need to be aware of this. You are compassed about with a cloud of witnesses, so you have no secret life to live anymore! In other words, you have become a public figure.

The 'cloud of witnesses' according to the above scripture includes an innumerable company of angels, as well as the spirits of just men made perfect such as Paul, Mary, Peter; and Jesus Himself.

Please be aware: It is not only the spirits of men who have gone ahead of us, the angels, God the Father, the Son and the Holy Spirit alone that make up the cloud of witnesses. Your co-workers, neighbors, and family members are part of the cloud of witnesses.

If you are a pastor's wife, your church members are part of the cloud of witnesses. They watch you day and night. They watch your character, relationships, behavior, presentations, dispositions etc.

If there is any area of your life therefore that you know you will be ashamed of if people got to know about it, you must work on yourself to ensure that such areas are straightened out on time with the word of God before it is too late, so you don't put yourself to shame. And in case your minister- husband makes reference to you in public in an illustration to buttress the word of God being preached, don't be offended or surprised. Remember that you are the closest person to him and you have no secret life to live anymore anyway!

Being aware of the cloud of witnesses and anticipating the results of their presence will save you from surprises, and unnecessary negative emotional response to them.

You must understand that just like in a natural race, the cloud of witnesses are free to make both positive and negative comments; you will definitely be commended and criticized, but you must refuse to allow their comments to get you distracted as you run the race. Both positive and negative comments can pose as distractions if care is not taken.

Ministry life is a life in the public eye. As expected therefore, you will be a victim of scrutiny. This has its privileges and problems. You will definitely be motivated by one or the other. You must ensure that you do not lose focus of your personal identity and calling.

Your behavior should actually be altered from inside out, not outside inn. This, in essence will improve your character positively; the other way round destroys your self-worth.

Positive Comments and Commendations

When people make positive comments about you and commend you as a minister's wife, don't let it get into your head and puff you up with pride or cause you to become haughty or arrogant. Many there are who started well but got caught up with pride which eventually became their un-doing in life and ministry.

Remember, pride is a silent killer! Pride, in essence is an over-estimation of self. That was what happened to Lucifer, a formerly anointed cherub and son of the morning (Isaiah 14: 12-20). Never fall into the trap of over-rating yourself! What more, God resists the proud (1Peter 5: 5).You shall not be destroyed!

Rather, let it humble you and make you appreciate the fact that God is at work in your life. The legend of faith, Oral Roberts was told by his mother in his early days in ministry: '...remain small in your own eyes...' This is very crucial. It is only then that you will enjoy more grace from God (1 Peter 5: 5). Constantly return all the glory unto Him; knowing fully well that without Him you can do nothing (John 15:5).

Also, beware of the sources of those 'highly-rated' comments! Truth is: some of those who are commending you highly today and 'shouting your hosanna' are the same ones tomorrow who would shout 'crucify him', if they have the chance.

So, seek God's commendation, not men; because in the ultimate, only he whom God commends is truly rewarded. This is the secret to fulfillment in life and ministry.

Negative Comments and Criticism

Negative comments and criticism on the other hand can bring discouragement. In most cases, its purpose is to distract you. Instead of getting discouraged, or develop hatred for such persons, what you need to do first is to examine yourself and ensure that those negative comments and criticisms are not true. In case they are true, see it as an opportunity for growth and development; take steps and begin to work on yourself to ensure necessary positive changes.

If those negative comments and criticisms about you are not true, refuse to get offended, intimidated, discouraged, or to develop hatred for the individuals concerned. Remember: *"woe unto you when all men shall speak well of you"* Luke 6: 26.

Keep in mind the fact that the devil is the source of all such, no matter the person(s) used. Remember Nehemiah!

Some people, especially women, through avenues like these give room to the spirit of bitterness. Remember that bitterness is not of God; it is of the devil. If indulged in, it can make you fail or fall short of the grace of

God. *Looking diligently lest any man fail of the grace of God; lest any root of bitterness springing up trouble you, and thereby many be defiled.* (Hebrews 12: 15).

To handle criticism, learn to forgive. You can even go a step further by praying for your offenders. Remember, when you forgive someone, your actions cannot be based on whether they have repented or not. Forgiveness is a gift that you have to freely give from the heart.

You may never hear an 'I am sorry' from your offenders; but when you forgive, things begin to work in your favor. The work of God committed to your care can progress and prosper. You can then serve God with a clear conscience and uncluttered mind. Interestingly, the grace of God becomes more real when you extend it to others. Ultimately, what the devil meant for evil God turns to good for you. You shall make it by the grace of God!

For an athlete who wants to win the prize for instance, while on the track he does not allow the comments and criticisms of the spectators to distract his attention. If he hears someone's comment about how short, thin, ugly or tall he is, he does not jettison the race to go and fight. Rather, he disciplines himself to continue the race and deafens his ears to such comments and criticisms.

Even when he hears people cheering him on, he does not respond to them or begin to dance on the field! Rather again, he disciplines himself to contain the excitement of the hour until he completes the race; or else while dancing on the field, someone else will overtake him and take his place in receiving the prize.

Discipline must therefore be your watchword as you run in this race so you can win the prize.

WHAT TO LAY ASIDE

> ***...let us lay aside every weight, and the sin which doth so easily beset us,."***
>
> Hebrews12: 1

In running a race, the athlete is taught among other things, how to lay aside any extra weight and be disciplined in order to be able to win the prize. Likewise, you as a minister's wife must lay aside certain things according to Hebrews 12:1 so that you can run effectively the race God has set before you.

You must understand that the words *"...lay aside..."* in the above scripture clearly indicates that it is your decision to lay these things aside, you choose whether to lay them aside or not. The responsibility to lay them aside is yours, not God's. What to lay aside includes:

Weights

The Good News Bible renders **Hebrews 12:1** this way: *"...let us rid ourselves of everything that gets in the way..."* Weights, obstacles, obstructions, disturbances and distractions; they all get in the way; they are hindrances. They may not be particularly sinful but the end result of a weight may cause you to sin, or slow down your speed of accomplishment or performance in the race.

'Weights' are not sinful in themselves, but you can do better without them. This is because among other things, they distract, obstruct and cause you to slacken in your commitment to God. The Bible says:

> ***All things are lawful unto me, but all things are not expedient: all things are lawful for me, but I will not be brought under the power of any.***
>
> 1 Corinthians 6: 12

The Good News Bible renders the above scripture more clearly; it says:

> ***...not everything is good for you I could say that I am allowed to do anything, but I am not going to let anything make me its slave.***

You must be able to choose the 'expedient' above the 'lawful'. Choose only what is good for you and don't let anything make you its slave.

For instance, don't allow television to enslave you to the point that you neglect your commitment to the Lord and the race set before you. Don't allow anything, even 'innocent' things like visitations, hobbies, family concerns or even children to prevent you from being committed to the Lord. It is when you have given God the first place that all other things like the aforementioned will fall in place.

For instance, watching too much television can become a weight if you now forgo your prayer time and word study for a time of leisure; staying 'glued' to your TV set.

> ***Every man that striveth for the mastery is temperate in all things.***
>
> 1 Corinthians 9: 25

"Temperate" in the above scripture means "moderate". Modesty must be your watchword. There are certain things other women may afford to engage in but you as a minister's wife cannot, no matter how 'harmless' they may appear.

Naturally, a man with a bag of cement on his head for instance; can by no means run a 100-metre race and win. Apart from the fact that his running will be a lot of difficulty; he will for sure have a head ache at the end of the day and definitely will be no match against those who are running lighter: he cannot win. The bag of cement though not sinful, constitutes a weight to him. This is exactly how 'weight' is.

Wisdom demands that you lay aside the weight of fashion craze, depression, frustration, discouragements, gluttony, comparison, laziness, stinginess, anxiety, etc and you will gain speed.

Sin

The second thing to lay aside is sin. Remember the scripture under consideration says:

> ***...and the sin which doth so easily beset us...***
>
> Hebrews12:1

It is evident from the scripture that every unrighteousness is sin, 1 John 5:17. Therefore any sin: whether 'big' or 'small' is sin, and must be avoided at all cost.

As a minister's wife, you should have nothing to do with things like adultery, strife, envy, lasciviousness, jealousy, stealing, hatred, fighting, covetousness, slandering, etc. All these and the like as listed in Ephesians 5:19-21, will not allow you to run the race effectively or win the prize. So lay them aside! Mortify them! (Colossians 3: 5).

Worthy of note also is the fact that the scripture says,

"...the sin that doth so easily beset us..." The phrase: "so easily beset" means to trouble constantly.

It is usually not the 'grave' and 'terrible' sins as some refer to them, like adultery, stealing, murder, and the like that trouble us; but the 'little' sins as some would call them like strife, unforgiveness, bitterness, a loose tongue, anxiety, stinginess, anger and the like.

These are all little foxes that can spoil your vine. Remember the scriptures command us to:

> ***Take out the foxes, the little foxes that spoil the vines: for our vines have tender grapes***
>
> Songs of Solomon 2: 5

The race God sets before you can be likened to a vine with tender grapes while bitterness, stinginess, gluttony, unforgiveness, anxiety and the like are all little foxes that have the capacity to spoil that vine. Be aware: 'little sins' give room to 'bigger sins', which subsequently apparently become a besetting, sin.

You know, as far as God is concerned, there is no 'big' or 'small' sin. 'Sin' is 'sin'; however you tend to categorize them. 'Small' as it maybe, it can lead to a shipwreck of one's faith which may eventually terminate in hell fire itself.

You will be surprised to know how many have been speedily ushered to an early grave(spiritual and physical);

due to 'besetting sins' such as anxiety, hatred, stinginess, fear, unforgiveness, bitterness, etc. which do not easily expose their captives.

Do not be one of those who think that way. If you are a worrywart, a doubter, or are in unforgiveness, fear, strife or have problems with anger; don't keep on accommodating it, lay it aside. Don't let it stop you. Stop it before it stops you. Sin has a deceptive nature (Hebrews 3: 13), so don't ever think that it doesn't matter.

How To Run The Race

All that has been discussed so far are the necessary preparations to be made in order to run the race. These things need to be known, understood, and appropriately dealt with.

However, in running the race there is a way, technique, a manner, which will grant you speed. You must know the 'how to' in whatever you want to do in order to gain speed.

The scripture in Hebrews 12:1; has not left us ignorant of the 'how to', but says:

...let us run WITH PATIENCE the race...

Before you can run with patience though; to start the race at all, you need the key of **faith**. 'Running' in this context implies you taking steps forward to get closer to your goal, destination or desired result.

First, it takes faith to run any race. You must believe that if you run, you can win. If you ask every athlete on the track, the reason he's there is because he believes he can win the race. The Bible says: *"it was faith that made Abraham obey when…He left his own country without knowing where he was going"* (Hebrews 11:8).

It takes faith for you to leave your starting point to run the race God has set before you as a minister's wife. Faith is the ever winning, never failing force in the universe. You must believe that the Lord who set this race before you will see you through.

Faith builds confidence in you towards God; and confidence in God has a great recompense of reward (Hebrews 10:35). In actual fact, faith is a practical expression of your confidence in God and His Word.

You must arm yourself with the weapon of faith. Primarily, faith in God; that *"…faithful is He that calleth you, who also will do it."* (Thessalonians 5: 24). Secondarily, faith in yourself; that you are well able and can run the race to the end successfully by the grace of God. Remember that whatever is not of faith is sin (Romans 14:23).

Secondly, you must add to your faith, **patience.**

Patience is a word that some people don't want to hear especially because of the wrong interpretation of it that many people have.

Patience means remaining consistent in the face of all challenges of life. It causes you to refuse to quit or give up. Patience however does not mean stagnancy, or lack of progress. It is the power of endurance, the ability to wait for the full results of what you desire. While you have not yet seen the full result, you are making satisfactory progress towards reaching your goal.

A natural athlete for instance, patiently endures the inconveniences of the hour as he runs on the track, making satisfactory progress by taking one step at a time as he moves towards his goal.

The scripture admonishes us to be:

> ***...followers of them who through FAITH and PATIENCE inherit the promises.***
>
> Hebrews 6: 12

It takes a combination of f**aith** and **patience** to obtain. Patience makes you to consistently apply your faith until you run the race to the end. Outside of faith, patience is barren.

You have to run the race both by faith and with patience, if you must obtain. You cannot afford to be too much in a hurry! Else, you will expend all your energy at the start off and will be left with nothing to complete the race.

Don't be in a hurry to be in your 'tomorrow' today, else you will find nothing in your tomorrow when it comes. You became a minister's wife five (5) years ago; no matter how much faith you possess, it is lack of patience that makes you want to be like someone who has been a minister's wife twenty (20) years ahead of you – in grace, unction, establishment, finance, experience, and even in other areas.

For lack of patience, many have made a shipwreck; you shall not! It is a race that you must run, but faith must be coupled with patience at all times.

Running, pursuing, taking it one step after another by faith coupled with patience; to obtain the perfect, future goal that God has for you: so He can hand you the prize, for obtaining that goal set before you.

You will obtain in Jesus name.

At this point, it is important for me to clearly state here that; not all ministers' wives will end up on the pulpit, in full time gospel preaching ministry. But God has a plan for your life. You must be able to locate your place in the kingdom and stay there fulfilled.

That you are a minister's wife does not automatically make you a pulpit, full time, gospel, preacher; but God had ordained that you live a fulfilled life, all the same. Please note that this does not mean that you will never stand behind a pulpit to preach, but it is just that it is not what you do on a full time basis.

Take for an example: the great woman, late Mama Oretha Haggin was the wife of the great faith legend, the late Dr. Kenneth Haggin; both of blessed memory. She was a most successful minister's wife, yet not in full time gospel pulpit preaching ministry; her ministry as it were is embedded in her husband's.

Same with some other great women of God like late Mama Evelyn Roberts, wife of the great legend, Chancellor Oral Roberts; Mama Theresa Cerullo, wife of Dr. Morris Cerullo; among many others who were successfully married and fulfilled and yet not in full time gospel pulpit preaching ministry.

Yet, there are others such as Mama Gloria Copeland, wife of prosperity giant, Dr Kenneth Copeland; who is a most successful minister's wife but is also in full time gospel pulpit preaching ministry: faithfully serving the Lord. Kathryn Kuhlman is another example of a successful woman minister, not just a minister's wife. There are many more of such. Each of them located their place in the kingdom and stayed true there.

I'm most grateful to God Almighty that I have located

my own place in the kingdom of God as a minister's wife, and by the help of God staying true to it; making my own little contributions as enabled by God. It is so very important for you to locate God's plan for your life and pursue just that.

FOOD FOR THOUGHT

"The man who wakes up and finds himself a success has not been sleeping."

Wilson Mizner

Chapter 5

Dealing With Loneliness

And he came thither unto a cave, and lodged there; and, behold, the word of the LORD* came *to him, and he said unto him, What doest thou here...

And he said ...and I,* even *I only, am left...

1 Kings 19:9-10

The above scripture describe the plight of a lonely soul, a minister of the gospel for that matter! Many have gone into a 'cave' and they are lodging there emotionally, psychologically and even spiritually. They could be surrounded by people but they feel lonely. They are not happy, in some worse cases like Elijah; some would prefer to die.

I have discovered that ministers' wives are not left out. They are confronted by loneliness. They have many people around them but no familiar face. They engage in so many conversations yet no one to 'talk' to. Painfully, in most cases at such times, their husbands are actively involved in the work of the ministry!

Everyone, including myself, at one time or another has had to deal with loneliness. But the good news is: you can overcome it rather than it overcoming you! You are not there alone, it is common and there is a way out.

> ***There hath no temptation taken you but such as is common to man: but God* is *faithful, who will not suffer you to be tempted above that ye are able; but will with the temptation also make a way to escape, that ye may be able to bear* it.**
>
> 1 Corinthians 10:13

Let me state clearly here from the onset that loneliness is completely different from being alone. One is required and is a blessing while the other has to be dealt with squarely if you desire to be effective as a minister's wife.

The *American Heritage Dictionary* defines **"alone"** as "Being apart from others." You could be alone without being lonely. Adam was alone in the garden but he was not lonely. As a matter of fact, he was not even conscious of his aloneness, until God himself decided to do something about it.

The scripture records several instances when Jesus was alone. He deliberately craved aloneness. He would often depart to the mountain alone to pray or get away from the people. For instance, in Matthew 14:23,

> ***And when he had sent the multitudes away, he went up into a mountain apart to pray: and when the evening was come, he was there alone.***

Also, in John 6:15,

> ***When Jesus therefore perceived that they would come and take him by force, to make him a king, he departed again into a mountain himself alone.***

The scripture says, ***"... he departed again."*** That means it was something he did quite often. Certain encounters are not possible except you are alone!

The Bible says:

> ***And Jacob was left alone; and there wrestled a man with him until the breaking of the day.***
>
> Genesis 32:24

Jacob could have ended his destiny as a "supplanter," save that he had that encounter because he was alone. That encounter gave him a name-change that opened up his destiny. His name was changed from Jacob to Israel.

> ***And he said, Thy name shall be called no more***

> ***Jacob, but Israel: for as a prince hast thou power with God and with men, and hast prevailed.***
>
> Genesis 32:28

Often times, it is when you are alone that you can see certain things that the hustle and bustle of activity won't let you see. Aloneness gives you an opportunity to observe vital things that otherwise could be clouded and neglected.

> ***And when even was come, the ship was in the midst of the sea, and he alone on the land.***
>
> ***And he saw them toiling in rowing; for the wind was contrary unto them: and about the fourth watch of the night he cometh unto them, walking upon the sea, and would have passed by them.***
>
> Mark 6:47-48

Jesus saw His disciples toiling and He went to them walking upon the sea. This provoked Peter's faith that made him also walk on the sea. From this encounter, as believers, we have come to learn that nothing shall be impossible to them that believe; for as long as your focus stays on Jesus and not on the situations and circumstances around you, you are sure to overcome even the forces of nature (Matthew 14:28-32). That is a lesson that would never had been learnt if Jesus was not left alone to see them toiling.

Loneliness, on the other hand, is a painful awareness that you lack meaningful contact with others. It involves a feeling of inner emptiness; a sense of feeling unloved and rejected by those around you, which may be accompanied by discouragement, sadness, a sense of isolation, restlessness and an intense desire to be wanted and needed by someone.

If unchecked on time, it may lead to depression due to an inability to cope with the facts of life. This was what Elijah the Prophet experienced when he ran away from Jezebel.

> ***And he came thither unto a cave, and lodged there; and, behold, the word of the LORD*** **came** ***to him, and he said unto him, What doest thou here, Elijah?***
>
> ***And he said, I have been very jealous for the LORD God of hosts: for the children of Israel have forsaken thy covenant, thrown down thine altars, and slain thy prophets with the sword; and I,*** **even** ***I only, am left; and they seek my life, to take it away.***
>
> 1 Kings19:9-10

The *American Heritage Dictionary* defines loneliness as a state of one "Without companions; dejected by the awareness of being alone." The *Oxford Advanced Learners Dictionary* defines it as a state of "being unhappy because you have no friends or people to talk to. A situation or period of time that is sad and spent alone."

Loneliness is one of the things that many ministers' wives often battle with. This is because by the nature of your calling as a minister's wife, you may find it difficult to make friends beyond mere acquaintances. You are a *"mother to all,"* and you find out that there is an unwritten law that precludes you from having favorites. So, when your minister husband is not available, there seems to be no one to share your personal concerns and experiences with.

Why Loneliness?

By God's design, we all have an innate need to love, be loved and belong. As children, we learn to give and receive affection and are taught the skills that will help us find acceptance in the society. Through our relationships with family, friends, co-workers and others, we form our sense of individuality and find our place in the mosaic of life. It is when that need for affection and fellowship goes unfulfilled, that we become restless, unhappy and lonely.

Types of Loneliness

Research shows that there are basically three kinds of loneliness. These are emotional, social and existential.

Emotional loneliness involves a lack of a psychologically intimate relationship with another person or persons. Naturally, and in keeping with our nature as companions, most women like to have their husbands around most of the times. I am sure you can relate to that; you want to see him around as much as possible, to tell him all about your experiences, your fears, doubts, plans etc, or to just be alone together enjoying his presence!

Unfortunately, your minister husband is much too mobile for that; traveling, attending meetings, services, conferences, studying, praying and generally being about his father's business! This creates a kind of emotional loneliness. You do not have close friends and yet your minister husband, the only one with whom you can closely relate with emotionally may not be readily available to you when you need him the most.

Social loneliness is the feeling of aimlessness, anxiety and emptiness. The society, particularly the African society, gives a minister's wife a certain unwritten code of conduct that expects her to be perfect at all times. She is expected to comport and conform herself according to certain standards. The societal expectations of her are so high that it triggers an anxiety to conform.

In some ministries and churches, she is expected to be a "mummy" that virtually turns her into an "Egyptian mummy." She must talk, walk and even dress according to certain standards. Her natural temperaments and preferences are rarely taken into consideration. Even the type of job or business she does, can be the subject of social scrutiny. The pressure to conform is so high, that her personal identity could be lost, if care is not taken.

Sometimes, society pressure can even make a minister's wife a hypocrite. When in public, she is one kind of a person; but, when at home, she is another. Living a life of double standards! Anything short of the expected standards provokes and may lead to abandonment. This can trigger loneliness if unchecked.

Existential loneliness is the sense of isolation which comes to someone who is separated from God and feels that life has no meaning. As a minister's wife, sometimes, your timing is not subject to your own control. The demands of the people can be so high, that you hardly have adequate time to develop and work on your own personal relationship with God. It is even possible for you to forget that you are first a Christian before a minister's wife.

Sometimes, before you even get out of bed, there is

somebody's issue already needing attention. It could be a phone call by someone who is in dire need of your prayer or counsel. By the time you are through with that, it may be time to attend to some other important issues such as getting the children set for school or attending to other household chores. Sometimes, it could even be a very bad news that upsets your entire day.

At some other times, someone may have a very bugging challenge and first thing in the morning, he or she is banging your door very early. Expectedly, like Jesus who could not resist the cry of mercy by blind Bartimaeus; you are compelled to stop whatever else you are doing, to attend to such a person. By the time you are through, the day is already in full swing!

Gradually and unconsciously, you are being robbed of your personal time of fellowship with the Lord. Sometimes, even the kind of study in the word that you undertake, is so geared towards meeting the needs of the people that you forget; it is ... *such as I have give I thee:* (Acts 3:6). You study to bless the people that you neglect your need for spiritual nourishment.

If not promptly dealt with, this could eventually lead to existential loneliness - separation from God. This is utterly dangerous!

Dangers of Loneliness

The dangers of loneliness to a minister's wife are

enormous. They include but are not limited to the following:

Insensitivity and inability to hear God

If loneliness is not dealt with, you can come to a point where you become so spiritually insensitive and find it difficult to hear God on certain issues that relate to you, having itching ears (2 Timothy 4: 5). This explains why the Bible says:

> ***For this people's heart is waxed gross, and their ears are dull of hearing, and their eyes they have closed...***
>
> Matthew 13: 15

Many times, this may get to a point when your emotional state can rob you of your personal fellowship with God. You begin to hear more of yourself in this state than you hear God.

This is a very dangerous and bad state spiritually, especially for a minister's wife. The enemy can take an advantage of this deplorable state to strike; so, be careful.

Inability to love yourself

It is possible that you get so sold out to the people that you forget to love others only as much as you love yourself (Matthew 22:39). You deny yourself of spiritual nourishments just so long as the people are blessed and "the work" is prospering.

This is an outright misplacement of priorities which ultimately can trigger loneliness and a feeling of personal isolation from God.

Loneliness is much more than an inconvenience. If left unchecked, there is the danger of it developing into anxiety and depression. It is possible to become completely immobilized by feelings of self-pity and helplessness.

The stress imposed by loneliness leads to a weakened immune system which could lead to heart disease and other physical ailments. Some try to mask pain by oversleeping or over indulging in food. But that is not a healthy thing to do. Don't try to drown your loneliness. Deal with it and overcome it!

Lack of joy

Loneliness is a subtle thief that can steal your joy. You never find a lonely person that is joyful. Loneliness causes joy to wither away from your life (**Joel 1: 12**). When joy withers, life itself become unfulfilling and unproductive.

At the point of loneliness, there is a tendency of thinking on things that could rub you of your joy. Joy is a matter of the heart. Therefore, you have a responsibility to guard it jealously as the scripture says:

> ***Keep thy heart with all diligence; for out of it* are *the issues of life.***
>
> Proverbs 4:23

Your heart must be loaded with things that will not give room to loneliness. The scriptural prescription in the following passage will be most helpful in this case.

> ***Finally, brethren, whatsoever things are true, whatsoever things* are *honest, whatsoever things* are *just, whatsoever things* are *pure, whatsoever things* are *lovely, whatsoever things* are *of good report; if* there be *any virtue, and if* there be *any praise, think on things.***
>
> Philippians 4:8

The more you apply this biblical therapy, the farther you are from loneliness.

Ill Health

Loneliness dries the bones! When the bones are dried up, health failure is the end result. This is because loneliness breeds depression which in turn automatically ends up in ill health. If the devil can successfully steal your joy, it will be an opening for him to strike with sickness. This is why the Bible says:

> ***A merry heart doeth good* like *a medicine: but a broken spirit drieth the bones.***
>
> Proverbs 17:22

As a minister's wife, your must learn to guard your health jealously. Do not allow anything to tamper negatively with your health. Remember the saying: health is wealth!

Ill health, among other things can cause distraction in ministry. You cannot be effective if you are not healthy. You need to be healthy in order to function in any area of your life. Give no room to depression; let your spirit be alive and active.

It frustrates the grace of God upon your life.

You know, it is possible to frustrate the grace of God! This is clearly stated in the word of God:

> ***I do not frustrate the grace of God: for if righteousness come by the law, then Christ is dead in vain.***
>
> Galatians 2: 21

To frustrate the grace of God means not letting it have full expression; not allowing it to achieve as expected. One major way of frustrating this grace is by giving room to loneliness.

When you are given to loneliness, the grace of God

upon your life cannot find full expression; it is handicapped, so to speak.

The scripture says:

> ***Let thy garments be always white; and let thy head lack no ointment.***
>
> Ecclesiastes 9:8

The grace of God upon your life can be likened to the ointment that keeps you functional in your office as a minister's wife. So, you cannot function effectively without the manifestation of the grace of God upon your life. Loneliness can deprive you of the grace that you need to function effectively in your office. In all areas of your life, you need the grace of God. Apostle Paul said:

> ***But by the grace of God I am what I am: and his grace which* was bestowed *upon me was not in vain; but I labored more abundantly than they all: yet not I, but the grace of God which was with me.***
>
> 1 Corinthians 15:10

Whether you are on the pulpit, at home, in the office or on a journey; the grace of God will distinguish you as a minister's wife anytime, any day.

If loneliness is so deadly, how can it be dealt with? The good news is that as deadly as loneliness is, it can be adequately dealt with. Here, I will share with you some of the vital ingredients that have personally helped me as a minister's wife over the years in dealing with this issue; certainly, they will be of immense help to you also.

How To Deal With Loneliness

Read this scripture with me very closely:

> ***I looked on my right hand, and beheld, but there was no man that would know me: refuge failed me; no man cared for my soul.***
>
> ***I cried unto thee, O LORD: I said, Thou art my refuge and my portion in the land of the living.***
>
> Psalms 142:4-5

Make Jesus your best friend!

The primary spiritual way by which you can overcome loneliness is by maintaining a close, personal daily walk with God through Jesus His son. Let God remain your refuge, portion and strength in the land of the living.

Make Jesus your best friend! He is the only friend that sticks closer than a brother (Proverbs 18: 24).

Never mistake activity and busyness for closeness with God. Cultivate your relationship with Him consciously by spending time ministering to Him in prayer, praise and worship and also by studying the Bible to draw nourishment, strength and encouragement.

Just like the biological family to which you belong, where you have a unique father-mother and daughter relationship; it should be the same spiritually. Walk and develop a strong relationship with God, so that when loneliness knocks at the door, you already have what it takes to deal with and triumph over it. Those who have developed a strong relationship with God, never have to be downcast with loneliness of any kind.

Personally, this is my greatest secret to dealing with loneliness and I can tell you; it works! Replace depressing feelings with God's everlasting truth such as Apostle Paul said in 2 Timothy 4:16-17:

> ***At my first answer no man stood with me, but all men forsook me: I pray God that it may not be laid to their charge.***
>
> ***Notwithstanding the Lord stood with me, and strengthened me; that by me the preaching might be fully known, and that all the Gentiles might hear: and I was delivered out of the mouth of the lion.***

Make Jesus your bosom friend, He never fails; He is always there and can be relied upon. Your minister husband is not and cannot be the source of your contentment. God alone can reach down to the very depth of your being and fill you with the divine joy that will terminate all loneliness and depression.

Be grateful!

You can never be truly great in life and ministry until you learn to be grateful, primarily to God and secondarily to man. So, rather than succumb to loneliness or feel miserable, allowing all kinds of negative thoughts to flood your mind; draw strength from God, while maintaining a grateful attitude that your husband is chasing God rather than women! Your husband is doing a beautiful and commendable work.

Remember that the scripture says:

> ***How beautiful upon the mountains are the feet of him that bringeth good tidings, that publisheth peace; that bringeth good tidings of good, that publisheth salvation; that saith unto Zion, Thy God reigneth!***
>
> Isaiah 52:7

Let that grateful attitude motivate you to rather pray for him the more, upholding him and the work of the ministry before the Lord on your knees. That way, you will not only be investing in the work of the Lord, but you will also have a sense of belonging; feel that you are a part of it. You will also experience your relationship with God getting better and better.

Start dwelling on the goodness of God

Consider how good God has been to you as a person. Take an inventory of your life, compare where you are to where you used to be and you will be surprised how good God has been to you.

Like the wordings of that great song writer: count your blessings and name them one by one and it will surprise you what the Lord has done!

The psalmist acknowledged that the fact that he even slept and woke up is because God sustained him (Psalms 3: 5). Dwell on the goodness of God!

The scripture says:

> ***Bless the Lord, O my soul, and forget not all his benefits:***
>
> Psalms 103: 2

Often, the things that we ought to forget are the ones the devil wants us to remember and the things we ought to remember are the ones he makes us forget; what a paradox!

The fact that you are a minister's wife is part of the goodness of God in your direction! Dwell on the goodness of God rather than on what you don't have or what you think He ought to have done but has not yet done for you.

Expectedly, the more you dwell on the goodness of God, the more of His goodness you see and experience. The reason why many people keep reducing in life is because they forget God's goodness.

This will definitely make a huge difference in your life and help in no small measure in effectively dealing with loneliness.

Keep yourself busy in service

You can overcome loneliness by keeping yourself busy in service. This includes service both in the family and in the ministry. Remember the common saying that the idle mind is the devil's workshop, your title or status notwithstanding. Until you keep yourself busy, the devil will keep whispering to you thoughts and ideas that lead to depression. See what Joshua had to do in order to be effective as a leader and overcome loneliness.

> ***This book of the law shall not depart out of thy mouth; but thou shalt meditate therein day and night, that thou mayest observe to do according to all that is written therein: for then thou shalt make thy way prosperous, and then thou shalt have good success.***
>
> Joshua 1:8

While Adam was dressing and keeping the garden, Eve was joblessly loitering around, until she became a victim of the devil's subtlety. That is why you must keep busy. Jesus, in one of His parables said: *occupy till I come* (Luke 19:13).

Apart from reading the Bible and other anointed materials, you can also invest in personal developmental studies. You can choose to study biographies of men and women in ministry or even advance your career. It may not necessarily be because you need the degree, but as part of the measures to ensure that you are gainfully engaged.

You can even undertake training in some handiwork of some sort. This could be very useful both in your home and in the work of the ministry. With it, you can undertake some creativity workshops and seminars in your local assembly that will be of tremendous benefits to other people.

For example, it could be in decoration from which your church decoration unit will benefit or children evangelism or any other area of your interest.

Fill your mind with thoughts of hope

To deal effectively with loneliness, you must be cautious what you fill your mind with. Please be aware that your life moves in the direction of your dominant thoughts. Your life will follow your thoughts. In essence, your thinking defines your living. This explains why the Bible says:

For as he thinketh in his heart, so is he:

Proverbs 23:7

Learn to focus on the positive things of life in your thoughts. In every situation, seek to see the right part of life.

Keep your hopes very high! Never allow thoughts of mediocrity. Be full of hope. Never allow any low moment, constantly remind yourself of the word of the Lord concerning you that clearly states that:

For to him that is joined to all the living there is hope: for a living dog is better than a dead lion.

Ecclesiastes 9:4

As long as you are in Christ Jesus, there is hope for you as a minister's wife; no matter the situation you may find yourself in.

Physical exercise

To deal with loneliness, you need to be active. Get involved in an exercise program. The Bible says:

For bodily exercise profiteth little:

I Timothy 4: 8

Exercise, move: put the law of movement to work! It will make you feel better. The little profiting involved in exercise can greatly will improve your health and over-all wellbeing; lifting your spirits and boosting your confidence.

Let go of unrealistic expectation

In dealing with loneliness, it is crucial to do away with all expectations that are unrealistic; about the ministry, your person, the family, etc.

Release your husband from having to meet all your needs! He is your companion, not the source of your joy or contentment.

You and your children as well as other family members should deliberately find a means of fitting into your minister husband's busy schedule. This will make life fulfilling.

Be real! Be practical! Enjoy the journey!

Engage yourself in a fulfilling venture

Lack of fulfillment is the reason why many are lonely. Fulfillment comes only when you pursue divine purpose. You must invest in discovering God's purpose for your life and engage in the pursuit of it. Life without purpose can be very empty and frustrating.

Don't keep your treasures buried in the ground, get involved! Kingdom service is a great way of being involved in your husband's ministry. Locate a service group where you can actually contribute to the growth of the ministry or church.

You can be involved in evangelism, or editorials – writing tracts, handbills, transcribing testimonies etc, or sanctuary keeping that helps to ensure the church building is always kept clean.

You can minister in schools or be gainfully employed either pursuing a career or business, fulfilling your God given purpose in life. You can even have an outreach for instance, to the poor and needy around you or visit orphanages, etc.

As I close this chapter, let me sound a note of warning here. In your quest to overcome loneliness, do not eliminate your need for your husband as this could affect your relationship. He is your husband and nothing should be allowed to take his place in your heart and life.

Engage the mysteries of the kingdom –the blood, feet washing, Holy Communion and the anointing oil, - to deal with any issue or anything that will negatively affect or hamper the maximal utilization of your time together.

With **the blood of Jesus**, purge your heart from every form of offence or feeling of neglect or rejection. They are dead works that could tamper negatively with your relationship. The Bible says:

> ***For if the blood of bulls and of goats, and the ashes of an heifer sprinkling the unclean, sanctifieth to the purifying of the flesh:***
>
> ***How much more shall the blood of Christ, who through the eternal Spirit offered himself without spot to God, purge your conscience from dead works to serve the living God?***
>
> Hebrews 9:13-14

The **feet washing** mystery was designed to release joy unto us anytime we engage in it.

> ***If I then, your Lord and Master, have washed your feet; ye also ought to wash one another's feet.***
>
> ***For I have given you an example, that ye should do as I have done to you.***
>
> ***Verily, verily, I say unto you, The servant is not greater than his lord; neither he that is sent greater than he that sent him.***
>
> ***If ye know these things, happy are ye if ye do them.***
>
> John 13:14-17

You need a free flow of joy to enjoy your husband's presence. Don't keep a catalog of offences or complaint for these treasured moments. They are meant to be enjoyed. So, look forward to it with excitement by washing your feet and tapping into the grace and virtues that are released thereby.

The **Holy Communion** is also a mystery that will help you in times like this. The Bible says:

> ***As the living Father hath sent me, and I live by the Father: so he that eateth me, even he shall live by me.***
>
> John 6:57

The Father lives in perfect harmony with the Son, Jesus Christ and the Holy Spirit. So, crave for this perfect unity as you relate with your husband.

Engage the force of the Holy Spirit via the **anointing oil.**

> ***Thou lovest righteousness, and hatest wickedness: therefore God, thy God, hath anointed thee with the oil of gladness above thy fellows.***
>
> ***All thy garments smell of myrrh, and aloes, and cassia, out of the ivory palaces, whereby they have made thee glad.***
>
> Psalm 45:7-8

As you receive the oil of gladness, you bear a smell that attracts and is irresistible. Let your smell physically and spiritually be as that referred to by Isaac *...as the smell of a field which the LORD hath blessed:* (Genesis 27:27).

Finally, make the most of the privileged times you

have together, no matter for how long or short the duration and intervals. Instead of sulking or whimpering when you are with him, invest that time in developing a very healthy, happy and rewarding time with each other.

Celebrate him! Make him the object of your attention, respect and focus. At the end of any such times together, let him know either by sending him a card or a note or by your words fitly spoken, when you have the opportunity, how much you enjoy your time together. This will encourage him and make him look forward to such times with you.

As you put these to work, you will be able to effectively deal with loneliness.

FOOD FOR THOUGHT

"Real security can only be found in that which can never be taken away from you your relationship with God."

Rick Warren

Chapter 6

Maintain Spiritual Fervency

Not slothful in business; fervent in spirit; serving the Lord.

Romans 12: 11

God is a Spirit, the same way you are a spirit. Man is essentially a spirit being. He has or possesses a soul (which is also referred to in the Bible in most cases as the mind) and this spirit is housed in a temple that is called the body. It is only the temple of a man i.e. the body that can be seen with the physical eyes. So, the real you is the spirit that is inside you.

However, in order for you to be able to relate effectively with God who is your true heavenly father, you must become very conscious of your spirit nature; because this is the real, most important you.

More often than not, believers make the mistake of

paying more attention to the physical man at the expense of the real man. But remember that the real you – your spirit is within and invisible. The real you is your spirit and it is with it that you are able to relate with God, your heavenly Father.

To be spiritually fervent, you must give your spirit man correct priority. Your spirit should take priority over your mind and body. Often times, the physical is wrongfully placed above the spirit and mind; probably because it is the visible aspect of man and with it contact is made with the world around us.

But the truth is that before you can have fellowship with God and enjoy it, you must be conscious of the real you which is your spirit. When your spirit is in touch with your heavenly father, it reflects in all other areas of your life.

What then is spiritual fervency? It means to have a strong and sincere connection with God; to be in touch with God, who is your source of existence and sustainer; being linked up with your heavenly father from where you draw power for performance.

Please be aware: only those who are in touch with God can touch men on earth. Until you are in touch with your heavenly father, you never can touch any man successfully here on earth.

The word 'fervency' means 'intense'. **Spiritual fervency therefore can be defined as intense, strong, sincere and passionate devotion to God**.

If I may ask: Are you devoted to God? How passionate is your devotion to your heavenly father? Can your devotion to God be said to be intense, strong and sincere? Truth is: until your spirit man is on fire for God, there is no way you can affect or be relevant to the lives of men here on earth.

Your husband, the minister is involved in a spiritual assignment; it's not like taking up employment in one secular organization or the other. So, as a minister's wife, both you and your husband are involved in a spiritual assignment; therefore you cannot afford to be carnal at all. Assuredly, the cost will be far more than what you can bear!

My husband, Bishop David Oyedepo says: "you cannot successfully carry out a spiritual assignment in the energy of the flesh". If there is any one therefore whose spirit must be on fire for the Lord, if there is anyone who must be fervent in spirit; it should be you, so as to give no place to the devil.

Keep The Fire Burning!

Spiritually, you must not let the fire go out; rather, you should keep it burning. Remember the scripture says:

Where no wood is, there the fire goeth out: so where there is no talebearer, the strife ceaseth.

Proverbs 26: 20

It is one thing to kindle a spiritual fire, but another thing completely to keep it burning; refusing to let it go out. When a fire is kindled, the only way for it not to go out, quench or be turned to ashes; is by consistently putting in more wood, in addition to the existing one. At the same time, you will be required to keep fanning the flame.

The word of God is the spiritual wood. On a regular basis, you need to find fresh word; this is in addition to what you already have. Make it a way of life to search the scriptures, daily (John 5: 39); believing God for insight, light, revelation and entrance into things required for your day-to-day living.

Truth is: only those who seek are permitted to find (Matthew 7:7)! Remember: "...when thou hast found it, then there shall be a reward, and thy expectation shall not be cut off (Proverbs 24: 14).

Then, apart from adding more wood to keep the fire burning, you also need to keep fanning the flame. You need the ministry of the Holy Spirit to be able to do this. The Holy Spirit is the spiritual fan, whose help and ministry you cannot do without if you must keep the fire burning.

Talking about the Holy Spirit, the Bible says:

> ***Whose fan is in his hand, and he will thoroughly purge hiss floor, and gather his wheat into the garner; but he will burn up the chaff with unquenchable fire.***
>
> Matthew 3: 12

So, you need the help and the ministry of the Holy Spirit to keep the fire burning. He is available to help your every infirmity; or simply put: inadequacies! This explains why Romans 8: 26 says: "Likewise the Spirit also helpeth our infirmities: ..."

Enjoying the help ministry of the Holy Spirit is not automatic, however; you have to call for it. At any point in time when you need the help ministry of the Holy Spirit, you can call for it; He is a very present help in time of need (Hebrews 4: 16)! You can always call for the help ministry of the Holy Spirit on the altar of prayer.

Has it ever occurred to you for instance, even in your local assembly where you worship; that not everyone who comes to church is genuinely seeking God? Some are real agents of the devil, with wicked intentions; and it takes someone whose spirit is on fire to be able to identify such people, and put them where they truly belong.

Please, be awake! Quit slumbering! Be at alert! Of course, I am not suggesting that you become suspicious of everybody; or begin to wrongly accuse people that you do not understand: as agents of the devil. When you are spiritually sensitive, you will not walk in suspicion but precision; and all agents of the devil will automatically find your environment uncomfortable. You become a no-go area to them!

You just be on fire! You see, when you are on fire no beast will be comfortable around you by virtue of the fire that is emitting from your spirit man. Every 'beast' will become uncomfortable and will therefore jump out of its own accord!

So, you must be spiritually active; on a consistent basis: not on an on –and – off basis! Some there are who started actively but along the line became so inconsistent, inactive and 'cold' that their first love for God and His kingdom is nowhere to be found in their lives anymore!

Many that were 'first' are now 'last' and vice versa (Matthew 19: 30; 20: 16, Mark 10: 31, Luke 13: 30)! May your place in the kingdom not be lost!

Why The Need To Maintain Spiritual Fervency?

Why should I be spiritually fervent? You may ask.

Let us examine this at this point.

It is a commandment from God

To be fervent in spirit is a commandment from God to you (Romans12: 11)! It is not a commandment from man, but from God! So, when you are spiritually fervent; you are obeying the commandment of God. Therefore, it is not optional, it is mandatory. It is not an issue of convenience; it is a subject of commandment.

As expected, this commandment for spiritual fervency to you from God is for your good; not God's! The scriptures in 1 John 5:3, makes it very clear that God's commandments are not grievous. God's commandments are not meant to grieve us, but to groom us; to prepare and get us set for the place where we ought to be in destiny.

So, when you are spiritually fervent; you are obedient to God's commandment. Be not deceived, only the willing and obedient are permitted to eat the good of the land (Isaiah 1: 19)!

When you obey God's commandment, you gain command!

The whole world lies in wickedness (1 John 5:19)

We live in a wild, wide world! The earlier you realize

this, the better. There is no doubting the fact that the whole world lies in wickedness. The scripture says:

> ***And we know that we are of God, and the whole world lieth in wickedness.***
>
> 1 John 5: 19

Nothing can be plainer than that. Since you are '…of God…', your best bet is to be spiritually alert in this world; since you are physically present in it. If you must therefore remain here and be relevant in your assignment, being spiritually fervent is not optional.

This assignment that you are into goes beyond what physical eyes can see, my dearly beloved sister! Don't only see and operate with your physical eyes alone; be spiritually connected.

Until you are spiritually connected there is no way you can walk 'safe', victoriously, in this wicked world. It is a wide and at the same time wild world; whether you believe it or not. This is because the devil is still the god of this world. 2 Corinthians 4: 4.

In the wild life, there are all kinds of animals; some of which are very dangerous. Your security is to have a proper guide.

Many years ago, my family and I visited a wild life park in one of the African countries. All kinds of animals that you could imagine were there. On arrival, we had to employ the services of a guide; he was very versatile and had a good working knowledge of the place. From time to time, we were given some vital safety instructions. We had to obey the safety instructions, so we had a wonderful stay.

In the same vein, in this wide and wild world; your security is for your spirit to be on fire so you can be divinely guided by the Holy Spirit.

So you can be connected to your source

And who is your source? God! For the Bible says:

> ***I am the vine, ye are the branches: He that abideth in me, and I in him, the same bringeth forth much fruit: for without me ye can do nothing.***
>
> John 15: 5

Any branch that will bear fruit must of a necessity be connected to its source; the vine. In the same vein, you must be connected to God; your source.

It is spiritual fervency that gets you 'hooked' up to your heavenly Father. Through fervency of spirit you are in touch with Him and as a result it becomes easy for you to be in touch with fellow men in this wild world and still be in charge and relevant too.

Spiritual fervency gets you rooted, it gets you

connected, and linked up to your God because there is a relationship between you both.

You need to be aware that whatever wants to break your relationship with your heavenly father wants to destroy your destiny. Whether it is the works of the flesh or whatever, it is targeting your destiny: don't allow it.

The Bible states categorically:

> ***Ye are of God, little children, and have overcome them: because greater is he that is in you, than he that is in the world.***
>
> 1 John 4: 4

Be conscious of the fact that the one who lives in you is greater than the one in the world! So you are not only an over comer but you are more than a conqueror; if and only if you are spiritually fervent and on fire for God, refusing to walk in the energy of the flesh.

So, when the enemy comes in like a flood (Isaiah 59: 19) and wants to get you involved in strife for example; because someone has wronged you: understand that the enemy is trying to find an inroad so he can disconnect you from your heavenly Father.

Remember that God warns that you should give no place to the devil.

Neither give place to the devil.

Ephesians 4: 27

If you give a place to the devil, you will be opening up your destiny to his attack and destruction. Your destiny shall not be destroyed!

For productivity and impact

Your productivity and impact in life is highly dependent on your spiritual fervency. Emphatically, the Bible says:

Abide in me, and I in you. As the branch cannot bear fruit of itself, except it abide in the vine; no more can ye, except ye abide in me.

John 15: 4

To abide in Him is to be spiritually fervent. As a branch therefore, the only way to be productive and impactful is to abide; be connected, fervent spiritually.

Spiritual fervency is a must, for you to be relevant and make impact in anyone's life in your lifetime.

How Do I Attain Spiritual Fervency?

If it is so important to be fervent spiritually, how do I attain it? You may ask. Let us examine this.

Recognize the need for it

It is only what you desire that you attract to yourself.

If you do not know what you need, then you have a long way to go. The Bible clearly states:

> ***But my God shall supply all your need according to his riches in glory by Christ Jesus.***
>
> Philippians 4:19

Whatever you do not see as a need, God is not committed to supply! Until you recognize spiritual fervency as a need, God cannot be committed to make it real in your life.

Rather than using this scripture to "claim" more clothes, shoes, cars, houses, etc. all the time; shift your gaze rather to spiritual things which when you are in command of, " ...all these things..." (Matthew 6: 33), such as clothes, shoes, cars, houses and so on, become additions.

Desire it

Whatever you do not desire, you do not deserve! Desire is a strong feeling that you want something. The Bible says:

> ***Delight thyself also in the LORD; and he shall give thee the desires of thine heart.***
>
> Psalms 37:4

God is committed to giving you only what you desire. Therefore, it is your desire that commits God to performance.

The importance of the power of desire in attaining spiritual fervency cannot be over-emphasized! Even Jesus, our perfect example had to put the power of desire to work. Before Jesus could eat the Passover with His disciples, He had to desire it (Luke 22: 15).

One important thing to note about desire in the above scripture is the fact that it is of the heart. It takes root, begins in the heart. And you know: God sees your heart, everything lay bare before Him. It is not enough therefore to express your desire for spiritual fervency in your words; from your heart, you must strongly desire it.

Interestingly, when the desire comes, it is a tree of life (Proverbs 13: 12)! And of course, with the tree of life at your disposal, you cannot but enjoy life to the fullest.

There is a pre-requisite, however, to God giving you the desires of your heart. You must delight in the Lord; let your life give Him great pleasure and satisfaction. Whatever does not give God pleasure or satisfaction in your life, should be avoided at all cost.

To be spiritually fervent, you must desire it; have a strong feeling that you want it.

Be determined

To determine something is to decide it. To be

spiritually fervent, you must be determined to do so. Be determined to be on fire for God.

Interestingly, determination is a personal decision. No one can decide for another. When you are determined to be on fire for God, He who sees your heart will ensure that it becomes a reality in your life by supernaturally enabling you to do all that it takes to realize it.

To be effective as a minister's wife, you need determination. Those who lack determination are easily discouraged and never accomplish anything worthwhile in life.

Daniel's life is a worthy of note here. Read the account of him here:

> ***But Daniel purposed in his heart that he would not defile himself with the portion of the king's meat, nor with the wine which he drank: therefore he requested of the prince of the eunuchs that he might not defile himself.***
>
> Daniel 1: 8

Daniel purposed in his heart, decided, determined, and God made it happen for him. No wonder, he and his colleagues were ten (10) times better than others! He was too much for the fiery furnace! He ended up above all, for the Bible says:

Then this Daniel was preferred above the presidents and princes, because an excellent spirit was in him and the king thought to set him over the whole realm.

Daniel 6: 3

Like Daniel, purpose in your heart that your spirit will be on fire for God from henceforth; and then God will make it happen for you.

Invest your time

Spiritual fervency does not just happen; you have to make it happen. For you to make it happen, you have to invest quality time. It is something you have to work at, if you desire it. You have to find out what it takes, and give it your all.

One of the things it requires is time investment. Many people spend time, very few invest it. Interestingly, everyone on earth has an equal share of it, daily - no one has more than another. What we do with it is what makes the difference.

Amazingly, spiritual fervency is not a gift! Don't waste your time seeking for the 'gift' of spiritual fervency. It doesn't exist! Every spiritually up-and-doing person you see is the one who consciously invests precious time into getting it.

Invest quality time in word study and prayer. Read

anointed books and materials that will open up your understanding, enlighten, encourage, challenge and keep you spiritually active and alert.

Remember, Daniel said:

> ***...I Daniel understood by books ...***
>
> Daniel 9: 3

So, determine right now to do away with time wasters in your life because time is a precious commodity that should be invested and not wasted.

Dissociate yourself from the company of time wasters and begin to invest quality time to your spiritual life. Remember, time is life!

Engage in spiritual exercises

Talking about the importance of spiritual exercises, the Bible says:

> ***But refuse profane and old wives' fables, and exercise thyself rather unto godliness.***
>
> ***For bodily exercise profiteth little: but godliness is profitable unto all things, having promise of the life that now is, and of that which is to come.***
>
> 1 Timothy 4: 7-8

The instruction here is that you refuse profane and old wives' fables. A fable is a short story partly based on fact. On the other hand, a profane person is one that is not spiritual. Instead, exercise yourself unto godliness.

One of the primary ways to exercise yourself unto godliness is through fasting. Fasting is a requirement, if you must be fervent as a minister's wife. This explains why the scripture says:

> ***Moreover when ye fast, be not, as the hypocrites, of a sad countenance: for they disfigure their faces, that they may appear unto men to fast. Verily I say unto you, They have their reward.***
>
> ***But thou, when thou fastest, anoint thine head, and wash thy face;***
>
> ***... and thy Father which seeth in secret, shall reward thee openly.***
>
> Matthew 6: 16-18

It is not a question of 'if ye fast', but it says: 'when ye fast'. This means that fasting is already part and parcel of the program if you desire to be spiritually fervent.

Many minister's wives have lost their spiritual fervency to uncontrollable eating; dug their spiritual grave with fork and knife!

They keep roaming around the cooker, microwave oven, fridge and the dining table at odd hours! Their mouth is always moving, always chewing something – at home, while driving, at work and even in the church!

Truth is; your eating pattern must be disciplined, even when you are not fasting.

The subject of fasting is not in the program of some at all. You cannot go too far, spiritually, that way! It is important for you to start to program for fasting, just like you program for eating. It should become part of your spiritual agenda.

This is not to suggest, however, that you should live a 'fasted life' and have an abnormal eating pattern. Remember: **"...wisdom is profitable to direct"** (Ecclesiastes 10: 10).

You must understand, however that your fasting does not and cannot change God; it only changes you as it mortifies the flesh and makes you more receptive to spiritual signals.

Prayer is another form of spiritual exercise that you must engage in, if you desire to be spiritually fervent. Prayer should become a way of life to you.

> ***But when ye pray, use not vain repetitions, as the heathen do: for they think that they shall be heard for their much speaking***
>
> Matthew 6: 7

Like fasting, it is not a question of "if ye pray", but "when ye pray". So, prayer is not optional, it is obligatory!

Learn to pray in your understanding as well as in the Spirit. This is because ... *the Spirit also helpeth our infirmities: for we know not what we should pray for as we ought: but the Spirit itself maketh intercession for us with groaning which cannot be uttered.* Romans 8: 26

Your prayer life must go beyond the level of asking for things to interceding for persons in need. You cannot be fervent spiritually until you can pray fervently! Remember:

> ***...The effectual fervent prayer of a righteous man availeth much.***
>
> James 5: 16(b)

Only those who know the secret of how to kneel before God in prayer succeed to stand tall before men. Truly, prayer changes things!

The good news is: both prayer and fasting carry open, undeniable rewards both here on earth and eternally in heaven. Notice the phrase: *...thy Father which seeth in secret shall reward thee openly*. Matthew 6: 6, 18. What a joy! If you have not been engaging in these spiritual exercises on a regular basis, you don't know what you have been missing! But, it is not too late for you to start right now.

Your fasting and prayer should always be coupled with the word of God. Outside the word of God, your fasting and prayer will be barren and cannot produce result. So, your prayer must be word-based; so also your fasting must be covered by scriptural provisions.

Truth is: there is a certain level of spiritual fervency that you cannot attain unto until you begin to engage in the spiritual exercise of prayer and fasting! Matthew 17:21.

Receive help from the Holy Spirit

Let me say categorically here: you cannot attain spiritual fervency without the help of the Holy Spirit. You will need the help of the Holy Spirit on a constant basis.

Bear in mind the fact that:

> ***... for by strength shall no man prevail.***
>
> 1 Samuel 2: 9

The good news however, is that help is always available for you from the Holy Spirit; all you need to do is to call for it. Please, be aware that until you call for His help, you cannot enjoy it. He – the Holy Spirit is your dependable helper.

If you are not baptized in the Holy Spirit with the evidence of speaking in tongues yet (Acts 2: 4), you need to do so. For you to be baptized; all you need to do is to ask Jesus the baptizer to baptize you and He sure will. It is that simple!

Work at it daily

Attaining spiritual fervency is not a once in a lifetime deal. On a daily basis you must take deliberate steps to build up spiritual momentum that will culminate in a life of spiritual vibrancy.

These truth examined above are the things I personally engage in, so as to maintain spiritual fervency and I can tell you; it works! God is no respecter of persons, so they will work in your life as well.

Give it what it takes. Take daily, practical steps to ensure that your spirit man is in shape. The benefits are numerous. Spiritual connectivity, productivity and fruitfulness are primary; among several others. I guarantee you, you will forever be grateful you did!

FOOD FOR THOUGHT

"You can not pursue a divine assignment in the energy of the flesh"

Dr. David Oyedepo

Chapter 7

Be Relevance-Conscious

> ***...and who knoweth whether thou art come to the kingdom for*** **such** ***a time as this?***
>
> Esther 4:14(c)

Before an inventor would put his hand to work, he would first sit down and think on the relevance of his product to his immediate environment and the world at large. In the same vein, when God put His hand to work at the beginning, everything that He created was connected and relevant to each other. There is nothing that was created that is not connected to other creation.

Relevance is defined to mean being useful to what is happening or being talked about. The consciousness of this truth is a driving force behind every productive idea, successful carrier, impacting ministries and effective individuals.

You Were Created To Be Relevant

When you were created as a woman, God did not create you as an appendage. This is contrary to popular opinion in the world today. Rather, He created you to be relevant in all areas.

Refuse to accept the idea that you were created to be a burden on His creation. Nothing can be farther from the truth!

The first woman was created to be a help that is meet for the first man. The Bible gave this account thus:

> ***And Adam gave names to all cattle, and to the fowl of the air, and to every beast of the field; but for Adam there was not found a help meet for him.***
>
> ***And the LORD God caused a deep sleep to fall upon Adam, and he slept: and he took one of his ribs, and closed up the flesh instead thereof;***
>
> ***And the rib, which the LORD God had taken from man, made he a woman, and brought her unto the man.***
>
> ***And Adam said, This is now bone of my bones, and flesh of my flesh: she shall be called Woman, because she was taken out of Man.***
>
> Genesis 2:20-23

You are not an afterthought of God's creation.

Remember that after God created everything in the book of Genesis and assessed His creation as very good, He now said – I believe: "Oh, there is a need to put a wonderful crown on my creation". He then went ahead and made you, the woman! That connotes relevance, honor and value. You are created for relevance, most especially as a minister's wife.

If created to be relevant, in what areas then? You may ask. Briefly, let us examine some of these areas where you are meant to be relevant.

Areas Of Relevance

Until you realize the opportunities and privileges you have at your disposal, you cannot be adequately relevant. Your position as a minister's wife is an enviable position. The position that many women wish could be theirs. If all you see is the downside of being married to a minister of the gospel, i.e. the challenges involved as well as the sacrifices you have to make, you will not be able to focus on being relevant in this highly esteemed calling of yours.

You are meant to be a woman of relevance to your generation. Anything short of that will be tantamount to an abuse of destiny and divine endowment. Areas of expected relevance include the following.

To Your Husband

Your primary assignment as a minister's wife is towards your husband, after God. Jealously guard and maintain an unbroken relationship with God; but at the same time, you must reverence the head He has placed over you-your husband.

The Bible clearly says:

> ***For the man is not of the woman; but the woman of the man.***
>
> ***Neither was the man created for the woman; but the woman for the man.***
>
> 1 Corinthians 11:8-9

Truth is: without the position of your husband as a minister, you couldn't have been a minister's wife. That clearly states therefore that your husband comes first before the ministry. Be a helper to your husband by getting involved in his life. You can get involved spiritually, physically and otherwise.

Be Spiritually Relevant. To be spiritually relevant to your husband, the following; they will be of immense help to you.

Pray for him

Prayer is a vital need for your husband as a minister. Every minister covets and appreciates being prayed for.

It is so crucial that Apostle Paul openly declared this request:

Brethren, pray for us.

1 Thessalonians 5: 25

There is no one that can intercede for him the way you could. When your hands are lifted up in prayers for him, you will see him having victories in the ministry.

When Israel fought against the Amalekites, their victory was as a result of Moses lifting up his hands. The bible records this account:

And it came to pass, when Moses held up his hand, that Israel prevailed: and when he let down his hand, Amalek prevailed.

Exoddus 17:11

Do not be caught up with so many other activities that you forget his dare need for your prayer. No one can pray for you like yourself; and you are both one according to scripture. The bible says:

...For this cause shall a man leave father and mother, and shall cleave to his wife: and they twain shall be one flesh

Wherefore they are no more twain, but one flesh. What therefore God hath joined together, let not man

put asunder.

Matthew 19: 5-6

Praying for your husband is in effect praying for yourself.

You can also exchange prayer points. For example, you can pray for him when he is about to take major decisions or when he is on a trip. Remember, his success in ministry is a plus to your life.

Get spiritual resource materials for him

To be successful in any profession, you require good, relevant and current resource materials. Ministry is a profession, it is a call of God and it is an honorable one. You must therefore learn how to go out of your way to source for and buy spiritual materials; this will help in no small measure to build him up spiritually. The Bible says:

> ***Study to show thyself approved unto God, a workman that needeth not to be ashamed, rightly dividing the word of truth.***
>
> 2 Timothy 2:15

God's approval of your husband's ministry depends on the impact he is making in the lives of people. Study materials are seriously required; so, do not get upset when you discover that he spends a lot of money on books.

Many years ago, my husband went on a trip outside the country. At his return, like any other wife; I asked for the things he brought back. He then took me to where his suitcase was and opened it, it was full of books!

If the contents of those books were understood and applied, they could make him become a manufacturer of all the other things that he could have bought on that particular trip; he said. The results are here today!

Without mincing words, we have one of the biggest and most current individual libraries in our home today. Encourage your husband to read and study.

Do not disturb his study time with unnecessary domestic affairs; respect that period and teach your children the same.

Search and discuss scriptures together

Reading books cannot take the place of reading the scriptures. The word of God is the ultimate; revelation from the word is what guarantees manifestation in ministry.

Read, study and discuss scriptures together; share your views with one another. Discourage every form of idle talk between you and your husband. The Bible says:

But I say unto you, That every idle word that men

shall speak, they shall give account thereof in the day of judgment.

Matthew 12:36

The Bible did not say with whom you speak the idle word; so, ensure your discussions are bible-based. Whenever you discover something new, share it and enjoy fellowship.

The scripture encourages us to mind edification in our discussions.

Speaking to yourselves in psalms and hymns and spiritual songs, singing and making melody in your heart to the Lord;

Ephesians 5:19

Discuss edifying issues and by so doing, you will be doing him good spiritually.

Give him Godly counsel

It is important for you to be sensitive to your husband's temperament. There are times when he will need your counsel on certain issues, you must be careful what kind of counsel you give; give him only godly counsel. Consider a woman giving this counsel to her husband:

Then said Zeresh his wife and all his friends unto him, Let a gallows be made of fifty cubits high, and tomorrow speak thou unto the king that Mordecai

> ***may be hanged thereon: then go thou in merrily with the king unto the banquet. And the thing pleased Haman; and he caused the gallows to be made.***
>
> Esther 5:14

If Zeresh had known that her husband will eventually end up on those gallows, she would not have given him the kind of advice she did.

If Sapphira had not conspired with her husband (Acts 5:1-11), perhaps the two of them would have been spared. That is why you have to be careful what you encourage your husband to do.

To be in a position to offer him godly counsel, you must be full of the word of God yourself; be spiritually sensitive and do not act on impulse. Take care not to be carried away with your husband's feeling, but tune to the Holy Spirit's direction and leading.

> ***For as many as are led by the Spirit of God, they are the sons of God.***
>
> Romans 8:14

You are a child of God, let this reflect in the type of counsel and advice that you give to him.

Be Physically Relevant

Man is made of spirit, soul and body. Your minister husband is spiritual, but he still lives in an earth suit -

the body. In as much as you are conscious of his spiritual well being, you must also pay attention to his physical well being. Consider the following tips, they will be helpful to you in being relevant to him physically:

Prepare good food for him

Food is very essential to the well being of a man. When God created man in the garden of Eden He made adequate preparation for their feeding

> ***And God said, Behold, I have given you every herb bearing seed, which* is *upon the face of all the earth, and every tree, in the which* is *the fruit of a tree yielding seed; to you it shall be for meat.***
>
> ***And to every beast of the earth, and to every fowl of the air, and to everything that creepeth upon the earth, wherein* there is *life,* I have given *every green herb for meat: and it was so.***
>
> Genesis 1:29-30

Good food is essential for good health as it helps a man to think well and energizes. It is your duty to find out what is good for him.

Many minister's wives have neglected this important aspect and have totally left it to house help. This could become a danger spot in the home, if care is not taken.

Do not starve your husband! At the same time though, you should not over feed him, balance is the key here.

Remember that a hungry man can neither be effective nor productive.

There was an account in the bible whereby hungry soldiers were sent to the battle field, the Bible records:

> ***Then said Jonathan, My father[1] hath troubled the land: see, I pray you, how mine eyes have been enlightened, because I tasted a little of this honey.***
>
> ***How much more, if haply the people had eaten freely today of the spoil of their enemies which they found? For had there not been now a much greater slaughter among the Philistines?***
>
> ***And they smote the Philistines that day from Michmash to Aijalon: and the people were very faint.***
>
> 1 Samuesl 14:29-31

Please be aware that physical food, just like spiritual one also has its place.

Encourage him to rest

Generally, most men are goal getters; so they end up becoming workaholics. They could be so carried away while at work and forget the need to take a break. Ministers are not left out; it could even be more involving than those on a secular job because they are involved with other people. It then becomes necessary for you to encourage him to rest when you notice that he needs it. The Bible says:

And on the seventh day God ended his work which he had made; and he rested on the seventh day from all his work which he had made.

Genesis 2:2

Be interested in his job; get to know his schedules so that you could remind him of his important dates.

One other thing that could encourage him to come home on time and rest is to keep your home organized and inviting.

Many men, including ministers find it difficult to go home because of the dirty habits of their wives. Keep your home in good condition; eradicate unnecessary noise.

Be sexually sensitive

Be sensitive to your husband's sexual needs. Sex in marriage is not just for child bearing; it is an act that should be enjoyed and refresh the couple. Your body is to be cherished and enjoyed by your husband. It is not carnal it is one of the mysteries of marriage.

Apostle Paul wrote to the Corinthians concerning marriage:

Nevertheless,* to avoid *fornication, let every man have his own wife, and let every woman have her own husband.

Let the husband render unto the wife due benevolence: and likewise also the wife unto the husband.

The wife hath not power of her own body, but the husband: and likewise also the husband hath not power of his own body, but the wife.

Defraud ye not one the other, except* it be *with consent for a time, that ye may give yourselves to fasting and prayer; and come together again, that Satan tempt you not for your incontinency.

1 Corinthians 7:2-5

Do not subject your husband to temptation outside by your insensitivity; be sexually sensitive. Make your bedroom inviting, look good when your husband is at home; do not take things for granted, and give no room to the devil.

Take good care of his wears

This is the description of the wears of a virtuous woman and her husband. The Bible says:

She maketh herself coverings of tapestry; her clothing* is *silk and purple.

Her husband is known in the gates, when he sitteth among the elders of the land.

Proverbs 31:22-23

This is the description of a well dressed woman; she

cannot pass without being noticed. Interestingly, her husband was not left out. For him to have been known when at the gate with the elders is a proof. If necessary, help him out with his color combinations.

Make sure he appears neat at all times. Sow this as seed into his life and ministry and you shall be rewarded.

> ***He that receiveth a prophet in the name of a prophet shall receive a prophet's reward; and he that receiveth a righteous man in the name of a righteous man shall receive a righteous man's reward.***
>
> Matthew 10:41

Be Relevant In The Ministry And To The Body Of Christ

As a minister's wife, you are called alongside your husband. Scripturally, both of you are one. This is why the Bible says:

> ***Therefore shall a man leave his father and his mother, and shall cleave unto his wife: and they shall be one flesh.***
>
> Genesis 2:24

You cannot be sleeping all day, thinking that after all your husband is the minister; called to do the work.

There are times when you will need to carry out one

ministerial assignment or another such as counseling and the like. It will be embarrassing if you are found lacking behind.

You must have to overcome fear and learn to communicate publicly. Develop relevant skills. Be transparent before one another and share things that will make meaning to his life and work.

Be spiritually current; update yourself in the things of God. See yourself as a minister and a vessel in the house of God. Get rid of every excess that might make you irrelevant in ministry. The Bible says:

> ***For we are his workmanship, created in Christ Jesus unto good works, which God hath before ordained that we should walk in them.***
>
> Ephesians 2:10

You are created to serve, created for good works, and to minister to others; irrespective of your gender. Let your gift compliment his call.

Your relevance should not just be to your husband's ministry alone, but to the body of Christ at large.

Positioning For A Life Of Relevance

To be relevant, there is a need for repositioning in your relationship with the Lord Jesus Christ. Also, you must have a good understanding of the assignment

God has committed into your hands. Constant repositioning, not once- in- a- life time repositioning is a requirement; if you desire to progress and not be stagnant.

Like stagnant water, many ministers' lives are 'stinking' as it were because they have refused to constantly reposition themselves.

The moon for example, always commands attention because of its splendor and beauty. Talking about the glory of the moon, the Bible says:

> **There is *one glory of the sun, and another glory of the moon, and another glory of the stars: for* one *star differeth from* another *star in glory.***
>
> 1 Corinthians 15:41

But as glorious as the moon is, it has no light of its own! The light that brings glory to the moon is the light of the sun and the only way the moon can enjoy the level of glory that it does, is by positioning itself at a right angle to the sun.

As long as the moon is correctly positioned to the sun, the moon reflects the light that comes from the sun. So, all the glamour, all that glory, all that attraction, that the moon enjoys is from the sun.

The Bible refers to Jesus as the Sun of Righteousness in Malachi 4: 2, *But unto you that fear my name shall the Sun of righteousness arise.* As a minister's wife, you can be likened to the moon. You don't have any power of your own but when you are in correct alignment with Jesus whom you are serving in the work of the ministry, you will begin to reflect His light (glory).

Please be aware that all the honor, glamour, respect, and beauty that come to you is because of your positioning to the Sun of Righteousness in the person of Jesus Christ. When you are correctly positioned and well aligned to Jesus, you become sought after and the scripture in Genesis 12:3 will be fulfilled in your life.

Requirements For A Life Of Relevance

To be relevant, certain requirements must be in place. You must be in the Spirit, maintain focus and be expectant. Let us examine each of them briefly here.

Be in the Spirit

Spirituality is the foundation for a life of relevance, any day! You cannot be more relevant than you are spiritual. To raise your level of relevance therefore, you have to raise your level of spirituality. This explains why the Bible says:

> ***For to be carnally minded is death; but to be spiritually minded is life and peace.***
>
> Romans 8: 6

Take time to go down the history lane (biblical and contemporary); you will discover that all those who were truly spiritual were relevant to their world. Truly, to be spiritually minded is life and peace!

The question then is: how spiritual are you? Interestingly, you know better! It's time to wake up and begin to work on yourself so you can mortify the deeds of the flesh and become more spiritually active!

The Bible says:

I was in the Spirit on the Lord's Day... and I heard...

Revelations 1: 10

If you are in the Spirit, you will hear God clearly. In other words, except you are in the Spirit, you cannot hear from God. For you to be in the Spirit however, you must be determined to disconnect yourself from the flesh because you cannot be in the Spirit and be in the flesh at the same time. The Bible says:

So then they that are in the flesh cannot please God.

Romans 8:8

Disconnect from the works of the flesh and every form of carnality. Don't operate and live your life based on how you feel, what you hear, or see all the time; that is carnality or living in the flesh. To be in the Spirit, you must leave the flesh alone. Carry out a self appraisal and see whether you are being entangled by the works of the flesh or not.

> ***For the flesh lusteth against the Spirit, and the Spirit against the flesh: and these are contrary the one to the other: so that ye cannot do the things that ye would.***
>
> ***But if ye be led of the Spirit, ye are not under the law.***
>
> ***Now the works of the flesh are manifest, which are these; adultery, fornication, uncleanness, lasciviousness, Idolatry, witchcraft, hatred, variance, emulations, wrath, strife, seditions, heresies, envyings, murders, drunkenness, revellings, and such like: of the which I tell you before, as I have also told*** you ***in time past, that they which do such things shall not inherit the kingdom of God.***
>
> Galatians 5: 17-21

You must deliberately disengage from the works and ways of the flesh, if you are going to be in the Spirit. Give no room to strife, envy, murmuring, reveling, hatred, etc.

Consciously refuse to indulge your flesh in what it enjoys doing, which of course will not allow the Spirit of God to manifest in and through you. The life of God will only radiate through you to others if you allow the Spirit of God within you to take control and steer your life.

How can you be in the Spirit?

How can I be in the Spirit? You may ask. Consider the following useful hints.

- Spend time studying the word of God, daily.
- Meditate daily on the word of God.
- Spend quality time in prayer.
- Pray more in the Holy Ghost- in tongues.

The life in the Spirit could be hindered if it is not daily guided. Apostle Paul said:

> ***For I delight in the law of God after the inward man:***
>
> ***But I see another law in my members, warring against the law of my mind, and bringing me into captivity to the law of sin which is in my members.***
>
> Romans 7:22-23

Take note and beware of the things that could hinder you from being in the Spirit from time to time, they include though not limited to the following:

- Wrong Association
- Feeding On Wrong Information
- Unforgiveness
- Bitterness

If you live in the Spirit, you will not fulfill the lusts of the flesh.

> ***This I say then, Walk in the Spirit, and ye shall not fulfill the lust of the flesh.***
>
> Galatians 5:16

This will greatly enhance your level of relevance which in turns will raise your effectiveness as a minister's wife.

Maintain a life of focus!

To be relevant in life, this is the second factor; you must maintain focus. Focus means concentration. The Bible says:

> ***If your eyes be single, your whole body will be full of light.***
>
> Matthew 6: 22

Focusing your attention on God and refusing every form of distraction will guarantee you a life of relevance. Divided attention is the undoing of many minister's wives. You need to pay full attention to Him so you don't miss His presence. For instance, you cannot be in ministry and in business at the same time; expecting to become a star in both.

That lame man at the beautiful gate of the temple would have missed his hour of visitation if he had not been focused.

The Bible says:

> ***And he gave heed unto them, expecting to receive something of them.***
>
> Acts 3:5

Your focus determines your expectation from God. He is the only one that can make you relevant in life. Evidently, Peter and John were focused on God, so, they had something valuable to give to the lame man. Peter said:

> ***but such as I have give I thee: In the name of Jesus Christ of Nazareth rise up and walk.***
>
> Acts 3: 6

May be the reason why you are still at the level that you are is because you are not focused. A life without relevance can be likened to spiritual lameness. But as you focus fully on God, He will straighten you out; healing you of spiritual lameness in every area of life and cause you to live a life of relevance as a minister's wife.

Hindrances To Being Focused

To be focused, you must deal with certain hindrances; cardinal among which are distractions and procrastination.

Distraction: Anything that wants to take your attention from the right thing is distraction. Many things will be there to distract you on a daily basis from focusing on being a person of relevance. As legitimate and important as sleep is, it can also be a form of distraction; if not properly tamed.

For sure there will be many lawful and legitimate things competing for your attention on daily basis, things like: children care, counselees, household chores, commitments here and there etc. You must learn to balance things appropriately.

There is no excuse for being busy without achieving your primary goal. There was this young man that was given an assignment but he was careless because he was busy 'here and there'. The Bible recorded this account:

> ***And as thy servant was busy here and there, he was gone. And the king of Israel said unto him, So* shall *thy judgment* be*; thyself hast decided* it.**
>
> 1 Kings 20:40

As expected, this man was judged. You need to learn to prioritize and remember you can only do so much; you cannot be all things to all people no matter how hard you try.

Procrastination: Leaving till tomorrow what can be done today.

Don't leave till tomorrow, what you can do today.

Whatever you can do today, do it today. Do today, what is in your power today to do and then when tomorrow comes, God will give you the enablement to do what you ought to do tomorrow.

Be Expectant

To be relevant in life, the third factor that must be in place is expectation. Be expectant! What you don't expect, you never experience. Expectation is said to be the mother of manifestation.

Jesus asked blind Bartimeaus:

> ***What wilt thou that I should do unto thee?***
>
> Mark 10:51

In other words Jesus was pointing out to him the need for the blind man to put his expectation in place. In the same vein, now that you understand the need for you to live a life of relevance; what do you want Jesus to do for you? You need to give expression to your expectation, like blind Bartimaeus did.

The Master is there with you as long as your heart is right with him, but what you do not expect you cannot experience. God can use you beyond your wildest imagination. The Bible says:

> ***...the desire of the righteous shall be granted.***
>
> Proverbs10: 24

But what if the righteous has no expectation? Then God has nothing to grant. So, get back on track and put your expectation in place. Please be aware: you are not here just to occupy space, but to prove your worth in the kingdom of God; for you ... *can do all things through Christ which strengtheneth you!*

FOOD FOR THOUGHT

"The measure of life is not in its duration, but in its donation."

Peter Marshall

Chapter 8

It's All About Responsibilities!

We have already established that being a minister's wife is a privilege from God and an incomparable one at that. All privileges though have responsibilities attached to them, which must be strictly adhered to for the privilege to be enjoyed and not abused.

Examine this scripture closely. It says:

> ***...For unto whomsoever much is given, of him shall be much required: and to whom men have committed much, of him they will ask the more.***
>
> Luke 12: 48

Imagine! God, Almighty has invested something in you that He believes you can use for the benefit of the body of Christ. You must appreciate that by rising up to the occasion and fulfill the attendant responsibilities of that awesome endowment.

So, what are my responsibilities as a minister's wife? You are probably asking. Come along with me as we examine some of them in this chapter, under the following sub-headings:

Responsibilities Towards:

- Husband
- Children and family
- Husband's ministry
- Local church
- The body of Christ at large

Towards Your Husband

Let us start from your responsibilities to your husband, courtesy of whom you occupy the honored position of a minister's wife. It goes without saying that no other profession or vocation in life requires the thriving of the husband-wife relationship to succeed, as ministry.

The type of husband-wife relationship that exists between the minister and his wife, both in secret and in the open goes a long way to determine how successful the minister operates in his calling.

Little wonder that one of the basic requirements outlined in scriptures for would-be leaders in the house of God was a stable, exemplary family life (1Timothy 3: 4-5).

Charity they say begins at home. It is critical to the survival and well being of the work of the ministry that a healthy relationship exists between your husband and yourself. I cannot emphasize this point enough and I believe you are seeing it too!

Now, let's go into some practical details of how to make this work and enhance your relationship with your minister husband minister.

Love

You have the responsibility to love and care for your minister-husband spirit, soul, and body.

> ***But speak thou the things which become sound doctrine...The aged women likewise...that they may teach the young women to be sober to LOVE their husbands, to LOVE their children!***
>
> Titus 2:1-4(emphasis mine)

It is obligatory, not optional for you to love your husband, more so as a minister's wife; because you are to be an example to others, especially those who find it difficult to do so. Loving your husband is a commandment from God to you.

From the above scripture, for you not to love your husband is lack of 'sound doctrine'. It is so important for you to love him that the above scripture recommends for you to be taught how to do it. Your love for your husband must be reflective in all areas of life.

Do you know that love is visible? Wherever love exists, it can be seen and conversely, wherever it is absent, even a blind man can 'see' it.

In our home, we once had a wall hanging with the inscription: "love is not love until it is shared." I couldn't agree with that more! Love is all about sharing and giving in order to benefit the other person.

Here, the kind of love that I am referring to is not just a good feeling that motivates you to do something nice in response to a kind gesture from your husband. I am talking about deep-seated devotion to your best friend that compels you to lovingly look out for him and to do him good all the time, irrespective of how you feel.

Feelings cannot be relied upon as the most appropriate yardstick if you want to do right; in fact I doubt if Jesus "felt" like going to die a painful death on the cross for a bunch of people who deserved to die for their own wrongdoing! Yet love compelled him.

God so loved the world that He gave (John 3:16). Thus, if you so love your husband also; you will definitely give him your attention, time, care, etc, and share your entire life with him.

Dear minister's wife, how much do you love your

husband? If you truly love him, demonstrate it, live it, and let it reflect in your relationship with him. Your love for him and your demonstration of it express your support for him and his ministry in no small way.

Don't be fooled by his "strong" exterior, which you interpret to mean that he is ok and does not require any demonstration of love from you. He may not verbalize his need for love from you, but remember no one hates to be loved.

Since man is a triune being (spirit, soul and body) according to 1Thessalonians 5: 23, let us see how you should express love to your husband in these three core areas of his being.

Spirit

The Bible says:

> ***The heart of her husband doth safety trust in her so that he shalt have no need of spoil. She will do him good and not evil all the days of her life.***
>
> Psalm 31:11-12

You need to be God – fearing. Your fear of God builds confident trust about you in your husband because he knows you will do nothing to harm him since you are God-fearing and God directs you in all you do, and so you do that which builds him up and not tear him down.

Trust is a most valuable asset in any marriage that will blossom and last. So when there is trust between you and your husband, success becomes inevitable, the devil notwithstanding. Fear God at all times and exhibit the same in your day-to-day life. That is one very important way of expressing love to your husband in the realm of the spirit.

Next, find your place in the plan God has mapped out for him and function there. Many ministers' wives know their husbands are called, but don't bother to find out where they fit in to the plan God has for their husbands.

I particularly love this version of the scripture that says:

> ***Wives fit in with your husband's plan for if they refuse to listen when you talk to them about the Lord, they will be won by your respectful, pure, behavior, and your Godly lives will speak to them better than any words. Don't be concerned about the outward beauty ...be beautiful inside... That kind of beauty was seen in the saintly women of old, who trusted God and fitted in with their husband's plan.***
>
> 1 Peter 3: 1-3 (TLB)

Nothing can be plainer than the above!

Keep in mind the fact that your call is embedded, as it were, in his; you have been called alongside him. So find out where you fit in and give it your best shot.

In practical ways, do your best to add to the work in whatever capacity God enables you-prayer, evangelism, administration, secretarial duties, children and youth ministry, women's ministry, language interpretation, pulpit ministry, writing/publishing; the list is endless. Make a difference in your own little way in your husband's ministry.

Also, the scripture says:

> ***Open rebuke is better than secret love***
>
> Proverbs 27:5

So, another way by which you can express love to your minister-husband spiritually is by stopping anything that can cause him to turn away from God.

A minister needs protection from the wiles of the devil, which sometimes he may be unaware of by virtue of his being 'lost' in executing his assignment. This explains why the Bible says:

> ***Two are better than one...if they fall, the one will lift up his fellow.***
>
> Ecclesiastes 1:9-10

So, as a minister's wife, you demonstrate that you truly love your husband when you do that which protects him spiritually. This may be through your wise counsels, constructive comments, observations, prayer, etc.

To avoid this is to lack a demonstration of true love. Remember Sapphira (Acts 5: 1-10)? She failed woefully in this area, by failing to stand for the truth and give her husband the most needed wise counsel then; so both of them met their untimely death. Learn a lesson from them!

Never be afraid to point out areas and issues that require his attention and correction, for fear that he will be upset with you. Do not be a partaker of other's sins!

You don't have to condemn him, criticize him or be judgmental in your approach. Approach issues lovingly, constructively; not accusing him or be demeaning. Let the wisdom of God guide you with discretion and it will be easier for him to see issues from the correct perspective so as to make necessary changes.

Soul

You demonstrate love in this area to your husband in the following practical ways:

Study Him. Love always implies an interest in a person. You cannot really love someone without showing interest in his or her affairs. Pay attention to your minister-husband. Study his moods, reactions, temperament, likes and dislikes.

Find out what brings out the best in him and what puts him off; and then use the knowledge wisely in relating with him. Respect his differences, interests, etc. and give him the necessary space he requires to get his work done in a most efficient manner.

Remember that the Bible says: She looketh well to the ways of her household... (Proverbs 31: 27). The phrase: 'She looketh well' means she observes, studies, and therefore is knowledgeable about the situations surrounding her husband and household.

She is able to read in between the lines and know the best thing to do in each situation. To do this, wisdom is a major requirement. Whenever you are in need of wisdom, you can always ask in prayer from God (James 1:5).

Don't be an ignorant minister's wife!

Submit to him. 'Oh, not that word again!', you are probably thinking. It is because you do not understand that submission is potent! It is like a two-edged sword; without it there can be no way forward with your husband and at the same time, it is your secret weapon of power with him. Not to dominate and manipulate him, but to enable you get his attention and regard.

At the crux of submission is allowing your husband to take the lead in decision-making that has to do with your family and the work of the ministry to which he has been called, while you wisely and lovingly go along-side with him as a worthy partner; making your contributions and inputs as you go. This does not reduce you or your worth in any way. On the contrary, you earn love, respect and regard from your husband.

Submission is an act of love. You can't submit to someone you don't love. So, rather than argue over issues or destroy the atmosphere of peace between both of you; submit to him.

Love does not seek its own, so: *be beautiful inside, in your heart with the lasting charm of a gentle and quiet spirit which is so precious to God* (1Peter 3: 2). And also *"...seek peace, and pursue it* (1Peter 3: 11). The peace of your household is important, it especially aids your husband's ability to receive clear directions from God and to relax and think properly so he can make accurate decisions and take correct steps.

Respect him. This is something all men crave from their wives over and above everything else. God made them to respond to anyone who holds them in high regard.

Even when he makes mistakes, don't condemn and crucify him out-rightly; as your husband, demonstrate your love and give him respect regardless, while at the same time maintaining a stand for truth and integrity.

Some women have the habit to openly disrespect and talk down on their husbands, especially when they make mistakes. Remember: that was why Vashti was removed from being a queen (Esther 1)! Keep in mind the fact that your minister-husband is God's servant albeit still in an earthen vessel. Correction should be made with wisdom and in love.

Truth is: If you disrespect him, both of you will lose respect. Plus, *"...and the wife must see to it that she deeply respects her husband, obeying, praising, and honoring him"* (Ephesians 5: 33 TLB) It is only the respect you 'sow' that you will 'reap'.

Body

Expressing love to your husband in this regard entails the following:

Clothing. **Concerning this, the bible says:** *"She is not afraid of the snow...for all her household are clothed with scarlet"* (Proverbs 31: 21). **See to it that he is neatly, smartly and appropriately dressed at all times. If necessary, assist him in making correct color combinations as well as accessorizing-ties, belts, socks, cufflinks etc**.

Remember that a first impression is very difficult, if

not impossible to correct; plus, the way you dress is the way you are addressed. He doesn't need to have many clothes before you can do this, you only need to pay a little attention and let your God-given female ingenuity come alive! Take note that it is an indictment on you if your husband is always unkempt and ill groomed.

Cleanliness. No man appreciates filth. In fact most men run away from such, *so the bible says: "...teach the young women... to be discrete chaste, KEEPERS at home* (Titus 2:5). She *"...eateth not the bread of idleness* (Proverbs 31:27).

Ensure that he is neat always, inside and outside. His body, clothes, room, automobile and everything about him must spell cleanliness. Always keep your homes neat, including your kitchen. Never forget that cleanliness is next to Godliness.

Feeding. This is another very important area where you demonstrate your love bodily, to your husband.

If you truly love your minister husband, it will reflect in how and what kind of physical food you feed him with. Plan a good menu for his up keep physically. Do not entrust absolutely what he eats to someone else. It is part of your responsibility to ensure that he is well fed.

Recently, God opened my eyes to this scripture with

respect to this truth and it has changed my perspective altogether. I am sure it will bless you as well. God's word says: *"...who satisfieth thy mouth with good things: so that thy youth is renewed like the eagles"* (Psalm 103:5).

Do you know that when the mouth is satisfied with good food, it brings renewal – bodily health, mind and spirit? His youth can actually be renewed by what you feed him with. Feed him with what is good for him, not just what he likes and he will be kept fit physically and otherwise.

Do you desire that your husband keep looking young? I know you do! So, plan a good menu for him; within your available income, of course. You can be creative even with a 'not-too-buoyant' budget. What you feed him with determines how he looks. Learn to cook good meals.

Even though a woman's role is not only in the kitchen and should not be limited to it, it is worthy of note that running the kitchen is one of her major roles. Don't concentrate on the minors at the expense of the majors.

Every lady (woman), I believe; needs to learn how to cook good meals. You should also keep improving on what you already know. Personally, I have a menu book and I keep updating my knowledge with every available opportunity. Parents should also teach their children to do so.

Sad to say, many good looking ladies do not know how to cook at all these days! Many have not been so taught by their parents. This ought not to be so. Mothers especially must teach their children early enough in life the wonderful art of good cooking. This way, their husbands will not be disappointed in them.

For a woman not to know how to cook good food is a shame and a disappointment. When you learn especially as a minister's wife to cook good meals for your husband, his soul cannot but bless you. Give him not just what he loves, but also what is good for him; this will automatically compel his blessings in your direction. And your husband's blessings are one of the things you must covet in life. It is different from any other blessing.

There is an adage in this part of the world that says: "the way to a man's heart is his stomach." This adage is partly implied in the scriptures. There is a biblical illustration of this truth. It is about Isaac and his two sons, Jacob and Esau. The bible says: *"...make me savoury meat, such as I love and bring it to me, that I may eat, that my soul may bless thee..."* (Genesis. 27:4).

This story is quite revealing and illustrates the connection between good eating and blessing from the soul. Please understand: this does not mean that you should cause your husband to become a glutton, but whatever he eats should be well monitored by you. If he is well fed, he will easily overcome the temptation of eating just anywhere anyhow, at anytime.

Some women have lost respect with their husband, others have incurred their wrath while some have even lost their marriages; for their inability to cook good food.

How well do you feed your husband and with what do you feed him? Eve gave Adam the forbidden fruit to eat and opened up the whole creation to the enemy's attack.

Lack of good feeding opens up your minister husband to the risk of eating outside the home. If eating outside the home becomes a way of life to him, it may eventually become a trap. Many men have been captured that way by some Jezebels. Give no place to the devil.

The bible says in 2Corinthians 4:7 says: *"But we have this treasure in earthen vessels that the excellency of the power may be of God and not of us."*

You must constantly remember that this treasure (God's anointing upon your husband) is still in an earthen vessel (your husband's physical body). For the treasure to continue to be of use to humanity, the vessel (body) must be preserved and adequately taken care of. You have a major role to play here.

Except a vessel is well taken care of the treasure it contains, no matter how precious cannot be useful. The physical body is the earthen vessel. The gift of God is the treasure. Treasures are very valuable. A major way of caring for this earthen vessel is by what he eats.

Even though there are fast-food places in every corner and restaurants are everywhere these days; there is still nothing like good old fashioned home-cooked food! Yes, it is quite tasking; but that is part of your loving responsibilities to your minister husband. Do it joyfully!

You can pack lunch for your husband as he leaves for work in the morning, and or ensure that he eats something before leaving home. In the alternative, if it is possible and practicable, have meals delivered to him at work at break time; or better still, encourage him to come home for a meal during his break period where proximity and other logistic considerations permit.

This is your chance! Take care of that earthen vessel and the treasure inside will be released to be a blessing to the world, beyond your wildest imagination. Feed your husband with good food and you never can tell how much God will use him to bless his world.

With your available resources, plan a balanced diet

for him and the family. A good meal doesn't have to be expensive; it only takes wisdom in creatively putting together what you have to arrive at a nourishing and appetizing meal.

Communication. **As a minister's wife, you must learn how to communicate well with your husband and others around him. Proper communication is very important in establishing a right relationship.**

Never hide from him whatever is necessary for him to know. Be transparent one to another. Genesis 2:25 says: *"and they were both naked the man and his wife and were not ashamed."* **This is the order God approves. Share ideas one with another. Both of you must be in good talking terms and be able to discuss freely with each other. For proper communication to be in place, there must be sincerity and openness.**

Also note-worthy is the fact that your husband should be treated as God's representative, because he actually is; but know that he may have some weaknesses because he is still in this earth suit. The way you treat him is the way others will treat him.

In John chapter 4 we see how a prostitute brought a whole town to Christ; so also can you as a minister's wife. You have that ability and much more to draw people to Christ.

For example, Christ sent his disciples out (they represented the bride) and they spoke of Him and the kingdom. This drew many more crowds unto Christ.

The way you talk about him and treat him either upholds or downgrades him. So, as a minister's wife, even when he makes mistakes, the way you approach it is important. The virtuous woman's character in Proverbs 31 brought about this result: *"her husband is KNOWN in the gates, when he seateth among elders of the land."*

Physically

Physically, marital rights show love. As a minister's wife, you must ensure that your husband is not denied in any way his rights to you bodily. Lack of cooperation in this area has made many ministers to fall into the arms of seducers (1Corinthians7: 2-5). Allow your husband to receive satisfaction of his physiological need of sex from you. Sex in marriage is scriptural and not filthy. God created it.

It should not be used as a weapon against your husband nor to manipulate him, because Satan is always around the corner; seeking for how to gain access. If the devil gains access and he falls into temptation, not only will his ministry be soiled; but your relationship will be marred. Understand that men and women have different sexual needs and desires. Satisfy his sexual needs.

The purpose of sex in marriage includes: to express love, cultivate intimacy, provide pleasure, and to propagate the human race.

Take heed; don't be naive and give no room for other women to flirt with your husband. Don't be suspicious however; rather, be sensitive. Even though your husband is a minister, he still has flesh and blood. Learn to render unto him due benevolence.

As a minister's wife, you have no power over your own body, but your husband does. Wife, don't defraud your minister husband (1Corinthians 7: 3-5). Ensure that he is sexually satisfied by you. Before any abstinence, as the scripture says permission should be sought from your husband and that for only a short while; and come together again, so that Satan tempt you not for your inconsistency.

Children And Family

Even if you are still believing God for the fruit of the womb, this segment is also for you! The scripture says:

> ***Lo, children are an heritage of the Lord: and the fruit of the womb is his reward***
>
> Psalms 127:3

Children are a blessing from God and as a minister's

wife, you must see them as such; not a burden or a curse. Fulfilling your parental responsibilities is a demonstration of your appreciation for the blessing of your children. How your children turn out eventually has a lot to do with your input.

Let us examine some of these parental responsibilities.

Love

First and foremost a minister's wife must love her children. I know it may sound a little strange to admonish a mother to love her children, but even the bible enjoins us to do so. (Titus 2:5.)

You should love them in word and in your deeds. The first responsibility in loving them is to bring them up in the fear of the Lord. A child that you have not brought up in the fear of the Lord you cannot claim to truly love. This is the major test of love for a child and the following hints will be helpful in doing so.

Teach Them About God

The scripture says: *"Remember now thy creator in the days of thy youth..."* (Ecclesiastes 12: 1). But how can they remember him whom they have not known? The scripture also says: *"train up a child in THE WAY he should go: and when he is old, he will not depart from it."* Proverbs 22: 6. Jesus also said: *"I am THE WAY..."* - John 14: 6.

So, the primary responsibility to your children is to teach them about the Lord and the ways of the Lord. To do this, wisdom is required.

Concerning Samson, Manoah and his wife asked the Lord; *"...and teach us what we shall do unto the child that shall be born"* (Judges 13:8). God taught them how the child should be brought up. So, ask the Lord to give you wisdom in this area.

As ministers, your children ought to be good examples for others. Remember though that each child is unique. The scriptures have countless references indicating that children should be brought up to know God and walk in His ways. Some ministers' children grow up to be wayward and hostile to God, mainly because they were not brought up in the way of the Lord from youth. That must not be allowed to happen to your children.

Please be aware, however, that you must ensure that there is a healthy balance in raising your children. Don't let them be under undue pressure as 'minister's kids', to be on edge and never be themselves. Allow them to have normal childhood so that they don't grow up and rebel when they leave home.

Teach Them The Word Of God

> ***Therefore shall ye lay up these my words in your heart and in your soul, and bind them for a sign upon your hand that they may be as frontlets between your eyes and ye shall teach them your children, speaking of them...***
>
> Deuteronomy 11:18-19

You must teach your children God's word on various issues of life: prayer, the word, giving, study, relationships, forgiveness, etc.

For instance, I ensure that all our children start tithing from birth; also, they always take offerings along to church. In fact, they're so used to it that they can't attend any church service without a reasonable offering. It is a commandment for you to teach them, not an advice! It will yield great dividends tomorrow when they are grown and are on their own.

Teach Them By Example

Teaching can be both verbal and by example. It has been proved beyond any doubt that the most effective way to teach children and to leave a lasting impression on them is by example.

Live a daily life before them that is worthy of emulation. Whether you realize it or not, children are very sensitive and will usually pick the character and mannerisms of their parents.

> ***...Be thou an example...in purity***
>
> 1 Timothy 4: 12

Children are natural mimics. No matter what you teach them, they learn better by example. Children are a reflection of their parents. May you live a life worthy of emulation. Remember: "a good example is twice as good as a good advice."

Teach Them To Pray

They must be taught to pray. Hudson Taylor, one of the greatest men of God of his time had this report concerning his parents. They were God-fearing people and instilled the fear of God and the spirit of prayer in their children.

He recalled that when he was growing up, whenever his father wanted to pray, he would lock himself up with all his children and begin to pray. He said at first, being a child he would cry, wanting to go out and play. But later it had an indelible effect on him. He learnt much about prayer and its importance. This was radical love, that despite his cries his father, who knew what was good for his children, always went ahead to instill it in them.

Discipline

An integral part of love is discipline.

> ***For whom the Lord loveth he chasteneth and scourgeth every son whom he receiveth...God dealeth with you as with sons: for what son is he whom the father chasteneth not? ... if ye be without chastisement...they ye are bastards, and not sons***
>
> Hebrews 12:6-8.

It is clear from this scriptural reference that you cannot claim to love your children if you don't take time to discipline them.

Discipline means training, especially of the mind and character, aimed at producing self-control and obedience. Your child must be brought up in the nurture and admonition of the Lord (Ephesians 6:4).

Don't look the other way when your children do wrong; be consistent in insisting on right behavior and attitudes at all times and in all situations.

These are the first and major responsibilities of a minister's wife to her children in order to bring them up in the way of the Lord. There were many ministers in Bible days whose children were wayward, and did not walk in the ways of God, e.g. (1Samuel 3:13, 2:27-30). One cannot help but wonder what their mothers were doing!

God's intention for any minister is to bring forth a Godly seed (Malachi 2:15), seed that can even step into the shoes (calling) of their parents, but alas! Many are not fit. May that not be your own testimony.

Susan Wesley who lived two centuries ago and turned out two of that Generation's most dedicated ministers – Charles and John Wesley (as well as nine other children), had an interesting philosophy on rearing children. "The child who refuses to go to bed at night is the same child that refuses to learn scriptures and follow the Lord. And just as sure as I'd see that child went to bed, I'll see that child come to God." That is discipline! No wonder she reaped the fruit.

A wise man once said, "The best thing you can spend on children is time." Being too busy to attend to them is wrong. If you are too busy to attend to them, you are indirectly telling God you don't appreciate his gifts; gifts that so many others are looking and seeking desperately for.

Provision Of Needs

Children have spiritual, emotional, and physical needs. A minister's wife should ensure that the needs of her children in all these areas are met. This does not mean that she must be the one to make all the provisions available, but she has to ensure that they are met through the co-operation of her husband and herself.

Spiritual. The spiritual needs of children include a personal relationship with Jesus, Holy Ghost baptism, developing Christian character, the fear of the Lord, understanding God's will for their lives, etc.

These can be met by prayer, upholding them before the Lord until they are matured enough to do so. Even if and when they are mature, it is important that you pray for and with them.

Moses' parents exercised their faith on his behalf (Hebrews11: 23). Also by your faith your children are clean (1 Corinthians 7:14) and have access to salvation (Acts 16:31).

Learn to pray for and with your children.

Physical. Children also have physical needs. These include feeding, clothing and shelter.

Clothing: The bible says: *"She is not afraid of the snow... all her household are clothed with scarlet"* (Proverbs 31: 21). You must ensure that your children are properly and neatly clothed, warm clothes for cold seasons and light clothes for warm seasons; festive clothes for occasions and clean stay-home clothes for everyday use.

Don't allow your children dress shabbily. Neatness is next to Godliness. They don't necessarily need to have many clothes to appear neat. Simply take care of the available ones. Remember that a first impression matters a lot and cannot be erased.

Proper feeding: The scripture says: She ariseth also while it is yet night and giveth meat to her household ..." Proverbs 31:15.

Make sure they are properly fed. Ensure a stable diet for them thereby enabling them to grow up strong and healthy. You ought to cultivate in them proper eating habits.

Growing children need particular types of food to ensure healthy growth. Make sure they eat carbohydrates like rice, yam, and cassava-based products, bread, potatoes and the like for energy building.

In addition, feed them with protein-rich foods such as beans, meat, fish and eggs for body –building. Also include fats that can be found in palm oil etc, as well as fruits and vegetables.

As a mother, supervise your children's feeding habits. Very little of sugary pastries such as sweets and biscuits should be permitted as they can be harmful to their teeth. Whenever they take such foods however, ensure they brush their teeth immediately afterwards. Also, ensure your growing children eat at least thrice a day. This is essentially your motherly responsibility.

When your children are well fed, they will not be

tempted to cultivate the habit of eating 'junk food' just anywhere outside the home.

Emotional Needs. Children also have emotional needs. The family is a team, a work group and a mini-nation. Teach your children to work together.

Also as they grow to become teenagers, get to understand the emotional changes they are going through and be of help to them to properly manage and overcome such emotions.

Educate yourself on puberty, adolescence as well as sex education and use your knowledge to in turn educate them in advance to avert the embarrassment that many go through.

Ministry work is not an excuse to be ineffective at home or careless about your family's needs.

They should be taught how to live peaceably with their siblings as well as with other children. Relationships are very important.

In particular, teach them good manners such as talking properly and decently, essentials of comportment, how to behave in public, how to address people in wisdom, respecting elders and the rights of others etc. Never assume, teach them!

Education: As a minister's wife, you should not be ignorant about your children's academics. Be interested in what they are being taught in school. Even in their class grades, monitor their performance.

Help your children to set goals in their academics as well as in their choice of subjects especially in high school. Make sure they have good subject-combinations that will enhance their future academics.

Finance. The financial needs of your children should be adequately provided for. Remember: "*...children ought not to lay up for the parents but the parents for the children*" 2 Corinthians 12:14.

Teach them the proper use of money so they don't grow up becoming spend thrifts or stingy adults. Let them learn how to pay their tithes, give offerings to God and also how to give to those in needs.

Discourage them from borrowing. Let them learn how to use money correctly, never allowing it to become lord of their lives. Even monetary gifts to them must be wisely handled, no matter how small.

They can earn money from little jobs too. We must rescue our generation by teaching our children the virtues of the right use of money.

Statistics show that 90% of the children of wealthy people don't end up wealthy because they never worked for the money and so do not know how to spend it judiciously. They were neither taught nor disciplined on how to spend money, so they end up wasting it.

They should be taught how to save money as well. As they grow, teach them how to buy things; especially minor purchases. As they spend money, teach them how to keep accurate records.

Then, it is very important to teach them how to save money. As they grow, encourage them not to spend all at their disposal; instill in them the discipline to learn to save some.

These principles have helped me a great deal in my own life; you sure will find them useful too.

Believing God for the fruit of the womb

At creation, God initiated a covenant of fruitfulness with man (Genesis 1:28). Concerning you the scripture says:

> ***Thou shalt be blessed above all people: there shall not be male or female barren among you, or among your cattle.***
>
> Deuteronomy 7:14

You are by design a fruitful being. Fruitfulness is part of your redemptive right. The price for your fruitfulness has been fully paid. Nothing can prevent you from enjoying the divine blessing of fruitfulness as long as it is your desire.

You can stand on the platform of hearty kingdom service to commit God to your fruitfulness. Get rid of the obstacles of unbelief, opposition of science, traditions and philosophies of men. Destroy all alternatives and focus on God. Refuse to give room to the feeling of hopelessness.

With the weapon of knowledge (John 8:32), hold on to God's word on fruitfulness. Tame your thought, watch your words and discipline your disposition. Carry an overcomers' mentality, refuse to quit. Begin to give thanks in advance for your fruitfulness.

Your case for fruitfulness is settled. Never lose hope, the miracle working God is on your side! Congratulations!

Husband's Ministry

You must share and accept your husband's calling, visions, dreams and ministry as yours. Your minister-husband should be able to freely share his vision with you and enjoy your support and encouragement. The ministry of your husband is his God-given assignment and his first responsibility, which is to the Lord and to His purposes.

In Genesis, the first reason the Lord thought of a female for Adam was to provide a help that is "meet" (suitable) for him. Suitable enough to assist him in the assignment He (God) gave to Adam. (Genesis 2: 18.)

Your responsibilities towards your husband's ministry among other things entail the following:

Acceptability. As a minister's wife, you must be ready to accept your husband's calling and office as well as your new status.

The bible says:

> ***Can two walk together except they be agreed?***
>
> Amos 3:3.

You can't accept or agree with what you can't 'see'. According to you, he may not look like what God has called him; but the scripture says: *"Judge not according to the appearance, but judge righteous judgement"* (John 7:24).

You must have a good spiritual understanding, perception and assessment of him so you can both work together to achieve the set goals God has placed before him.

A step further is not only to accept but also to identify with it. Don't be a bench warmer or on the sidelines. Be involved in the ministry, at whatever level you can.

Identification. You must identify with your husband's calling. To identify with someone means to be a part of whatever they are involved in or to share in someone's ideas and opinions.

No matter your 'calling', identify absolutely with his calling. Don't dissociate yourself from him at all in any way. Your calling as it were must be embedded in his own, as I have already mentioned.

Support. Be a true supporter (privately and publicly) of his calling. Be his no.1 fan! This will create confidence in him and therefore encourage him to fulfil God's call.

This will also create confidence in the people over whom God has made him an 'overseer'. This can be demonstrated in various ways. These include but are not limited to the following:

Prayer. In Exodus 17:12, we see a good illustration of this. The Israelites had just left Egypt and were fighting a battle against Amalek.

The scripture says that Moses stood at the top of the hill and with the rod of God in his hand, he lifted up his hands and as long as it was lifted, the children of Israel prevailed. But when he put them down Amalek prevailed. So, Aaron and Hur had to get him seated on a stone and held up his hands, thus the battle against Amalek was won.

In the same vein, the ministry requires spiritual Aarons and Hurs who will uphold it so that, that which God desires concerning the ministry may be brought to pass (Isaiah 62:1,6-7).

You are the best person to play the role that Aaron and Hur played for Moses in the above scripture for your husband. Learn to pray for your minister husband and the work of the ministry.

Wise counsel. The Bible says:

In the multitude of counsellors there is safety
Proverbs 11: 14

Constructive comments from you, as the minister's wife is essential. You are the closest person to him and so he should be able to confide in you and trust you more.

You should let your counsel always be to build up, not to tear down or manipulate. Jezebel's counsels to Ahab were all destructive (1kings 19:1-2, 21:1-7), Saphira failed to give her husband counsel and so they both lost their lives (Acts 5: 1-10); but Esther's counsel to the king was for the building up of a nation and God's purposes (Esther 7:1-6). The choice is yours. Make the right choice, follow the footsteps of Esther; be all eyes and make constructive comments.

Comfortable home atmosphere. All men crave an atmosphere of peace in their homes, and ministers of the gospel are no exception.

Let your home be a place where he looks forward to returning after a day's job or a trip. Make it a haven of rest indeed from all the storms raging outside.

Make it a place to re-fuel emotionally, physically, and spiritually. Avoid chaos; rather, make it a place of retreat. Share prayer, worship, talk and testimonies. Let there be love, laughter, praise, joy, prayer, blessing and play among family members. Faith and fun must go together.

When there is peace and quietness, he will be able to hear God correctly and receive counsel, direction and instructions from him. (1 kings 19:9-13, 1 corinthians 14:33.)

Please be aware: Peace and quietness doesn't necessarily mean not talking at all in the home (although it is not beneficial to be too talkative), as there can be physical silence and yet tension and resentment in the atmosphere at home. It simply means having a cordial, agreeable and tension-free aura in the home.

It is the presence of a virtual tangible serene atmosphere in the home. A peaceful atmosphere must be cultivated and friction or tension must be avoided at all cost.

Keep in mind: "Where there is... strife there is CONFUSION and EVERY EVIL work" (James 3:16). You dictate the atmosphere in your home; that's how influential God made you.

Learn to overlook certain things that are not very important. Don't be petty, and do not be a nagger of your minister-husband. Allow peace to reign and be patient with his shortcomings, after all you are not perfect either.

Make your home conducive for the Spirit of God to operate in. Let the spiritual atmosphere be such that your minister -husband can receive from God at anytime. Make home a place where your husband will long to return to after a ministerial assignment etc.

Be Hospitable. *A minister's wife should be accommodating. Even if other women are not, you as a minister's wife should be hospitable; especially to those involved in the calling e.g. co-laborers, members of staff, church members etc.*

Concerning this, the scripture says: "*Distributing to the necessity of saints: given to hospitality*" (Romans 12:13). Hospitality is part of the calling.

When you are given to hospitality you distribute to the necessity of the saints. As a distributor of blessings, you will never lack blessings, and at the same time, you never lose your reward.

Many women are easily irritated. They are

unapproachable and explode in anger and resentment too easily. Rather than being one of such, be accommodative. Let your home be conducive for people to stay and get blessed.

By so doing, Sarah and Abraham entertained angels unawares and set pace for their long-awaited miracle. Little wonder the Bible instructs: *"Be not forgetful to entertain strangers; for thereby some have entertained angels unawares"* (Hebrews 13: 2). You can also do the same thing.

As people, especially ministers of the gospel stay in your home; they deposit more of God's anointing there and you can add all of that to yours to make a better you.

Read the story of the Shunamite woman in 2kings 4:8-10. She was referred to as **"a great woman."** What made her become a great woman? HOSPITALITY! Your greatness in life has to do with you level of hospitality.

If you are not hospitable, your greatness may remain a dream that may never be realized. This woman always constrained Elisha, the man of God to eat and tarry in their home.

She made her home a comfortable place for Elisha, the minister. No wonder her prayer was heard and she bore a son after many years of barrenness, according to the word of the prophet (verses10 –17). Not only that, her dead son was also raised back to life later on. Hospitality will make you more fruitful than you are right now.

Whenever a minister who stays under your roof blesses you, embrace such blessings and God will honor it. Your greatness, to a certain degree is tied to your hospitality.

Don't always eat all your food and drink all your water alone, sharing with nobody! Else, when need arises, no one may be there for you. Be welcoming and accommodating! Again, this must be done with discretion so as not to open the door to the devil and get trapped; especially in these dangerous days.

Personally, it is always my joy to welcome people, especially ministers into our home. Each time they come, I know they deposit some anointing and God's grace, which has always added to the grace of God in my home.

Right now, receive an impartation of the grace of God that is at work in my life and home for hospitality into your life and home now, in Jesus name.

Local Church

A minister's wife is known and read virtually by all

members of her local church. She is like an epistle to her local church, known and read by all.

You must be careful the kind of epistle you are to your local assembly. Learn to be a living example, worthy of emulation. 2Corinthians 3: 2 says: *"ye are our epistle written in our hearts, known and read of all men...."*

Your presence in the local assembly is not just for the purpose of being on the sidelines, but you should be involved.

Spiritually. *As a minister's wife, you must be spiritually awake; interested in the things of God and wanting to be a source of blessing to others. You should have a constant desire to grow in the things of God* (1 Peter 2:2).

As a minister's wife, you should not be 'cold' towards the things of God, especially when it comes to the affairs of the church. How can a fire be kept burning if it is placed in water? How can your minister -husband burn with the zeal of God if you are cold and indifferent to the affairs of the ministry or your local church?

The Bible says: "...who maketh...his ministers a flame of fire" (Hebrews 1: 7). *How can the congregation themselves be aflame if you, who is closest to the minister is cold and dry spiritually? The attitudes of the minister's wife provoke others either negatively or positively.*

As a woman, you have the power of influence vested in you. The influence you wield can either encourage the whole congregation or cause a lot of them to flee from the things of God and of the local assembly.

Relationships. *The word 'relationship' means 'connection'. You must learn how to relate properly to people around you in the local assembly. A healthy relationship must be built to make for a healthy body of believers. Busy -bodying or gossiping should be shunned at all costs (1Peter 4:15).*

In your local assembly, learn the art of relating in an appropriate manner with people at their own level in order to be a blessing to them. Whether it is a child, man or woman, young or old the ability to relate with them on a platform they can understand is necessary.

This explains why the scripture says: *"be of the same mind one toward another. Mind not high things, but condescend to men of low estate…'* (Romans 12:16) and *"Let nothing be done through strife or vainglory but in lowliness of mind let each esteem other better than themselves."* Philippians 2:3.

Even God could not help man until he found a way of relating with man, by sending His only begotten son to the world. You cannot be a blessing to someone without a connection of some sort.

Remember: *"If a man say, I love God and hateth his brother, he is a liar: for he that loveth not his brother whom he hath seen, how can he love God whom he hath not seen?"*

Your relationship with people paints pictures, either positively or negatively to the public. Learn to appreciate people and have healthy, meaningful relationships with them in spite of their shortcomings. Never over-estimate yourself.

Conversation. *There is a need to recognize the importance of the use of the mouth here. Its power can be used positively or negatively. The Bible tells us about the power of the tongue.*

> ***For I will give you a mouth and wisdom, which all you adversaries shall not be able to gain say or resist.***
>
> Luke 21: 15

From the above scripture it is evident that:

Your mouth is a gift from God. Take note of the statement:" *For I will give you..." in the above scripture. B*ecause it is God's gift, use it to glorify God who is the giver, or else He may be angry with you and withdraw his gift. When God withdraws His gift of the mouth from anyone, the words of that person no longer carry any weight.

It is a weapon of war: This phrase in the above scripture makes that very clear. ***"...a mouth...which all your adversaries shall not be able ...resist."*** Your mouth is not just for eating and drinking, it is a spiritual weapon that God has given you!

It should be identified with wisdom: The wisdom of the wise is revealed in the words of her mouth. The Bible says: ***"...She openeth her mouth with wisdom; and in her tongue is the law of kindness"*** (Proverbs 31:26). Your mouth reveals your wisdom level. How wise you are will be revealed by your conversation!

The minister's wife can run down the minister's work by her conversation. Conversely, she can also build it up through her conversation. "Words are like eggs", an adage says, "which once broken, cannot be put back together again."

Remember Jesus and the woman of Samaria whom he met at the well (John 4), and how the whole city gathered to see Jesus because of her words. So also, people can be made to gather and see what the Lord is doing through your husband's life and ministry by the words of your mouth.

Speak only those things that build up. You should always ask yourself, 'what I am saying now, is it up-building or a hindrance to someone? Will God be pleased? Can I say it in God's presence with a pure conscience; the Holy Spirit will be able to give you right answers to these questions.

Be chaste (pure) in your conversation. The living Bible renders the word 'chaste' as ***'clean indeed,'*** having pure motives which make for healthy conversation. Also, **"let your speech be always with grace, seasoned with salt, that ye may know how ye ought to answer every man"** (Colossians 4: 6). You must know how to answer each person that you are conversing with appropriately.

Appearance. You create a lasting impression at first sight. So, your appearance as a minister's wife must portray a responsible code of conduct; it must be radiant and show the love, joy and peace of God that already exist in your heart (1Peter 3:3-4).

You can be regarded as the spiritual mother or mother in Israel (2 Samuel 20:19) of your local assembly. You need to recognize it and be ready to live up to expectation. Your smile means a lot to people and your frowning also does.

Your appearance should portray neatness, cleanliness and modesty. To be excessively flamboyant and flashy may cause speculation and make people withdraw. On the other hand to be shabby, dirty and untidy makes you look irresponsible.

So, be nice and modest (Philippians 4:5). When you do this, you earn respect. Remember RESPECT IS EARNED, not imposed.

The Body Of Christ At Large

To the body of Christ at large, as a minister's wife you must be a worthy example to follow. You may not be known by all and sundry in the body of Christ, but the way you handle your present status goes a long way in determining how far you will go in future. Faithfulness in these little matters will definitely attract a lifting (Luke 16:10).

The most important thing is that each part of the body is supplying the necessary nutrients to cause the growth of the body at large.

So, even in your 'little' corner, make sure your actions (and sometimes inactions) are contributing to the progress and establishment of the body of Christ at large; and not hampering it in any way. The grace of God is more than sufficient for you in all these. Together, we shall make it!

FOOD FOR THOUGHT

"I must do something" will always solve more problems than "something must be done"

Anonymous

Chapter 9

The Key Of Submission

Wives, submit yourselves unto your own husbands, as unto the Lord.

Ephesians 5: 22

The word 'submission' to some may sound like drinking a cup of bitter herbs, or may cause a drop in the temperature of your 'praise level!' However, woman, it does not have to be so. If God commanded it, then it must be for your sake and there must be some benefits in it for you.

Submission is a vital key to unlocking the door to your effectiveness as a minister's wife. Without it, you may not be able to go far in life and ministry. We ought to have a good understanding of God's ways.

The bible says:

Good understanding giveth favor...

Proverbs 13:15

To be favored before God and be effective in your calling, we need a good understanding of this word: 'submission'. More so, as a minister's wife you are 'THE" example others will be watching out for. What is submission all about?

Submission is defined by the oxford dictionary as "willingly putting yourself under someone else's authority, or acceptance of another's power"

Though God sees you and your husband as equal before Him and having the same right- standing, He has commanded that the wife accept the authority of the husband over her, (authority here means: power to give orders and make others obey) from a willing heart not grudgingly, or with a complaining heart. *"Wives, submit yourselves unto your own husbands, as it is fit in the Lord."* Colossians 3:18.

As a minister's wife, to raise your level of effectiveness, you must take note of the following issues about submission:

God, who is a God of order, set the order of the trinity as Father, Son and Holy Ghost and none is greater than the other; yet He is known as three (3) persons in one (1), and in the above order (1 John 5:7). So also has he patterned the family in the order of God, Husband, Wife and Children!

It is necessary for you, the wife; to see, understand, appreciate, and practice this God- ordained order: in respect and honor of the Lord. When you observe this order primarily because you want to honor the Lord and show your respect for Him' the Lord is pleased with you; and when He is pleased, what good does He withhold? None at all!

Essentially, submission is a matter of the heart

For your submission to your husband to be meaningful, the starting point is the heart. Until it takes root in your heart, it holds no rewards and cannot last; you submit for a while and then revert to your former 'rebellious' ways. This ought not to be so.

If you battle with submission to your husband, it is because the word of God has not gained entrance into your heart. Let your heart be tender and receptive to the word of God, thereby increasing your level of effectiveness as a minister's wife from thirty-fold to sixty-fold, then to a hundred-fold (Luke 8:15)!

See it as a demonstration of your respect to Christ because it is Christ who set him (your husband) over you. If you do so, it will eventually find expression on the outside; not vice versa, because that will be eye-service.

If you despise your husband in your heart and pretend

to 'respect' him outwardly, it is hypocrisy. But when your submission to him starts from the heart and then reflects outwardly, then Christ is pleased.

You should be able to say to the Lord: "*As for me, in the uprightness of mine heart I have willingly offered all these things... unto thee* (1 Chronicles 29:17)." Submission that has no root in the heart is mere hypocrisy.

Submit in thoughts, words and actions

Your submission to your minister husband should be in your thoughts, words and actions.

Truth is: the state of the **thoughts** of your heart determines the words of your mouth. Even though thoughts are invisible, they are made manifest in your words and actions. Without a doubt, rebellious thoughts will lead to rebellious words and acts; you are actually what you think (Proverbs 23:7)!

You need to be aware however, that your thought life is greatly influenced by what you continually behold. Be careful what you watch read and listen to; separate yourself from and severe all links with any thing that is contrary to biblical principles.

The company you keep also has a way of affecting your thought pattern greatly. If I may ask: Who are your friends? Are they women who disrespect and do not submit to their husbands or vice versa? You must dissociate yourself from every unholy and unedifying relationship.

Wish your husband well, even in your thoughts, because that is where true, lasting and biblical submission begins!

Your **words**: the choice and presentation reflect the level of your submission. How do you address your husband? You can convey submission, rebellion, or indifference by your choice of words. Do not speak rudely or use derogatory words to your minister husband.

Learn to speak right and gracious words. This will in turn bring you into favor with your husband. Right words, when spoken at the right time are without a doubt of great value (Proverbs 25: 11).

Your **actions** should reflect submission. Practical submission is characterized by obedience; obedience is the key here. You cannot claim to be submissive to a husband that you disobey always. Don't always advance reasons why his view will not work.

The example of Sarah in the bible is that of a covenant woman whose lifestyle of obedience we are enjoined to emulate (Isaiah 51: 2). You will be doing what is right when you follow the example of Sarah because she obeyed and honored her husband Abraham as the head of the house (1 Peter 3: 4- 6 TLB).

Through her obedience, her name is included in the biblical hall of fame on faith (Hebrews 11: 11)! In God's record of hall of fame, your name shall not be missing.

Your submission must therefore be in thoughts, words and actions; for you to be effective as a minister's wife.

Submission is a commandment from God

It is a commandment from God for the wife to submit to her husband, and His commandments are not grievous (1 John 5:3). His commandment is life everlasting (John 12:50). His commandments do not bring burdens but blessings. Due to ignorance and inadequate understanding, some believers sometimes find God's commandments difficult to obey.

My husband, Dr David Oyedepo has said: "God's commandments are not to grieve you, but to groom you." This is very true! When you submit to your husband, God grooms you to become more effective and be your best!

Your submission to your husband is meant to be absolute

Submit to him in everything, as unto the Lord. It should be in all areas of life. It should cover your spiritual life, affect your finances, and involve your physical body as well as everything about you. There are certain outfits, for example that I do not wear, because my husband does not like them. It's part of my submission to him!

It is important for me to mention however that the degree of submission a man enjoys from his wife is determined by the degree to which he (the man) submits to Christ.

Husbands who want their wives to submit absolutely to them should also submit absolutely to Christ. Submitting to my husband therefore becomes easy because he is also walking in total submission to God and His word in all areas, particularly as it affects our relationship.

Submitting to a husband who does not submit to the authority of Christ will surely lead to disaster. If your husband wants you to get involved in some ungodly thing – stealing, lying, deceit, dishonesty, strife, and the like; it will be foolishness, not submission to do so. Remember what happened to Sapphira in Acts 5:1-11?

The Bible says:

> ***...why hast thou conceived this thing in thine heart? Thou hast not lied unto men, but unto God.***
>
> Acts 5: 4

Your destiny shall not be destroyed!

Your submission to your husband should stem out of your desire to obey the Lord

In essence, this means that if your submission to him on any given issue will contradict your faith in Christ and cause you to sin against him, you must decline. In other words submission does not imply foolishly obeying every instruction or desire of your husband. If what he wants you to do violate God's law in any way, then you must obey God.

However, this is not a license for you to be rude or shirk in your other responsibilities to him or the ministry; it must be done politely with all reverence coupled with discretion, your reasons clearly and prayerfully stated.

Submit to your husband in spiritual matters

As a minister's wife, you must first identify with your husband's calling or vision. Please be aware: it is unscriptural for a woman to seek to pursue a vision or a spiritual project if it is contrary to, or not in consonance with the husband's vision.

In actual fact, the Bible says:

> ***...Who trusted God and fitted in with their husband's plans.***
>
> 1 Peter 3: 5 (TLB)

So, you are expected to 'fit in'. Like a part of a jigsaw puzzle, you are to adapt and adjust to your husband's dreams! As you do this heartily and joyfully, God's great agenda for your life begins to open up in a greater dimension; and if God has given you a ministry, it will definitely not contradict your husband's, and he will gladly be in support.

God is not the author of confusion! He commands that everything should be done decently and in order (1 Corinthians 14:40). I guarantee it works; I am a living proof.

Some minister's wives even take offence if not allowed to take up certain activities in some meetings or their local church. Some resort to quarrelling, strife, envy, fighting, back-biting, and the like. This is very shameful.

Rather than resort to these shameful acts, if you know you have a genuine case, wisdom demands that you take it to God in prayers. Remember that prayer changes things!

Physically, submit to your husband

You need to understand that your body belongs to your minister husband and his to you; this will make it easier to yield your body to him.

For instance, you may not 'feel' like making love with your husband at a particular time, but out of submission, you freely do so if he so desires. Your husband may even go out of his way to make sure both of you enjoy it, and at the end of the day you'll be glad you did! This has happened to me several times. Plus, this could even make you earn more respect from him.

Whether he does or not however, your obedience to God's commandment in this regard will bring you so much satisfaction.

Also, don't keep your body away from your spouse with the intention of 'punishing' him; it is unscriptural (1 Corinthians 7: 3-5). Neither should you use this to manipulate him- yielding when you want to get something from him and vice versa; this will amount to harlotry, giving your body in exchange for a personal gain.

Physical submission also includes your outward appearance- both of your person in particular, and the home in general. With your person; your outfit, hair-do, make-up and the like should spell your submission to him. Biblical submission would not let you wear any of those in a manner that will displease him nor God.

On the home front: learn to take care of the home and keep it clean, also learn to cook well. Do not leave your house, especially the closet in a disorderly manner.

If there's a particular kind of meal that your husband likes, wisdom demands that you learn to cook it; as long as it is good and healthy for him, rather than say something such as: 'That is not how I learnt to cook!'

Submit to your husband financially too!

You and your minister husband ought to become one in the area of finance as well. Improper handling of money has become the undoing of many marriages, homes and ministries today. Money has become the god of many, exalting it above the Almighty God.

Many have the love of money rather than the love of God, so they deal dishonestly with people and with one another even in the home. Concerning this, the Bible states:

> ***For the love of money is the root of all evil: which while some coveted after, they have erred from the faith, and pierced themselves through with many sorrows.***
>
> 1 Timothy 6: 10

Some go to the extent of 'hiding' money from one another – in banks, investment and stock houses. Some women even acquire properties like houses, cars, and so on without the knowledge of the spouse. Nothing can be more dangerous than this! If danger strikes, everything in hiding then comes to the open and this could bring shame.

Money should never command your love! Improper money handling can make you err from the faith, lose ministry, get pierced with many sorrows, and ultimately end in hell! Shouldn't you take caution?

Bear in mind the fact that money is merely a medium of exchange; it is meant to serve you, not you serve it. Never let it become a channel for the devil to gain access into your family or bring division.

You must be financially faithful to your minister husband. Do not take the money that is meant for feeding to buy new outfit such as clothes and shoes for yourself and claim that the food money was not enough!

The solution is: Operate an open agenda, financially (Genesis 2: 25). As husband and wife, whether you keep a joint account or separate accounts, you must ensure that there is openness and transparency. It is the only way to avoid financial shame. This is the secret of the financial rest that we enjoy in our home and ministry; and I guarantee, it works!

Signs Of Submission

If you are submissive to your husband, the signs of submission will be seen in your life. These include, but are not limited to the following:

Prompt obedience to your husband's instructions. Whatever instructions he gives, you will willingly and gladly carry them out in good time, as long as they are not contrary to God's word or your conscience.

Profound respect for him: Your husband deserves your respect. If you respect him because he is your head, indirectly it is yourself you are respecting; and vice versa. Even if he makes mistakes, don't disrespect him. Rather, ask God for wisdom on how to make him discover the mistakes so as to make amends.

An integral aspect of respect is how you address and respond to him. Watch this and make sure that both privately and publicly, you give your husband high regard in the way you address him; especially if you are angry or are not having your way!

Humility: Acknowledge and appreciate his headship. Give no room to pride in your life. It has destroyed many homes, don't let it destroy yours. After all, the scripture says: **"see to it that you DEEPLY respect your husband, obeying, praising and honoring him"** (Ephesians 5:33 TLB).

Even if God's grace upon your life appears to be glowing brighter than your husband's, submission is the key that will keep it glowing brighter or else it will start dimming. After all, a woman is an extension of her husband. You are "Mrs. His name." He is your head and you are his crown (Proverbs12:4). Without your husband as head, where will you (his crown) be? The beauty of a crown is when it is on the head!

Lack of submission is very deadly; it can even make the Holy Spirit to withdraw. The sad thing about such a situation is that until problems begin to rush in like a flood, some believers are never aware that He has withdrawn. Do not wait until problems arise before you awake to the fact that your lack of submission to your husband grieves the Holy Spirit. Act fast. **Act now!**

Agreed: some men may be lacking in some areas, thereby do not make it easy for their wives to submit; while some husbands by their loving attitudes make submission so enjoyable. If your situation is like the first case, please note; you can't afford to break any of God's commands because someone else did. So, submit to your husband irrespective of whether he does his part or not.

Factors That Enhance Submission

There are certain factors that enhance submission, that is; they help you to walk in submission to your husband, irrespective of his actions or responses.

Abigail knew and had this insight, which was why

even her husband's foolishness could not bring evil on her family (1Samuel 25: 25). You can also operate these principles and they will definitely work for you. Let us examine some of them here briefly.

Prayer: There is tremendous power in prayer. Prayer does not only change situations (Acts 16:25-26), but it also brings deliverance (Acts 12:5-11) and changes people (Galatians 4:19). God himself can be moved in prayers (2 Kings 20:1-5).

Any issue on which you find it difficult to submit to your husband should be taken to God in prayer. As you pray about it, you will be amazed how grace for submission will be released to you.

Commitment: To enhance your submission, commitment is required. Be committed to your husband and to your marriage. If you're truly committed to your marriage, you will submit to your husband.

Commitment is a kind of stimulant. It stirs you up, makes you active or arouses you to be faithful to the command of submission; even when you don't feel like it.

Commitment can be verbal or written. It should be exhibited verbally to your husband like Joshua did to the Lord and the people of Israel declared it unto God (Joshua 24:14-24).

From time to time, communicate with your husband

and remind him of your marriage vows; it will certainly motivate him positively, especially if those vows were bible-based. This could also positively affect his commitment to make submission easy for you.

Sometimes, you can also make your commitment known to your husband in a written form, like God did to the Israelites (Exodus 20). Both ways will work wonders.

Benefits of commitment include the following:

It builds **a stronger relationship** between both of you. Your husband will be able to trust you more and thereby be able to share the mysteries that the Lord reveals to him to you. Also, when you express your commitment, it becomes an instrument through which the Holy Spirit builds a stronger love in his heart for you. Until you do take steps, the Holy Spirit won't act. Which builder have you ever seen who builds without necessary materials such as cement, sand, water and the like? In the same vein, the Holy Spirit needs you to take steps before He can act.

It brings fulfillment and glorifies God. These are part of the benefits of commitment. When you communicate your commitment, whether written or verbal; you commit God who in turn sees to it that all things work together for good in your marriage. By your commitment, you are honoring God: *...the Lord hath been witness between thee and the wife of thy youth...* (Malachi 2:14) Because He is the originator of the institution of marriage, when you accept and declare His principles, He is being honored (praised). This in turns bring you fulfillment. Does submission really profit? You may ask? Yes it does. The blessings of submission are numerous. However a few are:

A Covering

There is spiritual covering (protective shield) over you as long as you submit to your husband. Sarah enjoyed this covering when she was in the house of Abimelech. Because of her submissiveness to Abraham, God did not allow her to be molested.

It was wrong for Abraham to have lied, even though Sarah was also Abraham's sister (Genesis 20: 2, 12), but she was more of a wife to him than a sister. Sarah enjoyed divine intervention, which was much more result- oriented than Abraham, Sarah or both of them combined could have produced; all because of the submission and meekness of Sarah. (Genesis 12:10-20; chapter 20).

Promotion And Enthronement

Submission enthrones and promotes. Jesus, our

perfect example submitted to God by dying on the cross; no wonder he obtained a more excellent name from the Father than all. *He humbled himself...wherefore God also hath highly exalted him, and given him a name which is above every name.* (Philippians 2: 9). When you submit to your husband, you enjoy honor and promotion from God, your husband and others.

You Reap A Harvest Of Submission

Your seed determine your harvest. Every natural farmer understands this process. When you sow corn seeds, you reap corn; when you sow bean seeds, you reap a harvest of beans.

Submission is a seed. So, when you submit to your husband, it is a seed that you sow; and the scripture says: *...whatsoever a man soweth, that shall he also reap* (Galatians 8: 7). Therefore, "...do for others what you want them to do for you... (Matthew 7: 12 TLB)".

When you submit to your husband, others will submit to you in return; they will also easily submit to him because they see you do so. People will rebel and refuse to submit to you if you do not sow the seed of submission.

But you must keep in mind the fact that there is a time lag between planting and harvest time. You do not reap your harvest the day you plant your seed. The seed has to be tended, watered and nurtured; these have to be done patiently for it to grow and bring forth fruits.

It is the same way with submission. You have to keep nurturing the seed of submission over a period of time before you can begin to harvest it

As a minister's wife, if you do not sow seeds of submission to your husband, your children in particular and others in general will rebel against you (Genesis 8: 22).

If you see a minister's wife to whom people such as co-workers, subordinates, ministry staff, etc; especially women don't submit and whose authority they rebel against, most likely she's not submissive to her husband at home.

You Enjoy More Love

When you submit to your husband, he will love you much more (1Peter 3:1) and his praise of you will be heard by all men (Proverbs 31:28). Submission is like a magnet. It automatically magnetizes your husband's love to you. Woman, do you want more love from your husband? I know you do! Submission is the key.

You Become a Worthy Example

By your submission, your life begin to speak and

through this others are established; reason is because when people see the orderliness in your home, they're challenged by it (1Peter 3: 6; Esther 1:17). By this, you are lifting up a standard, positively for others to follow (Isaiah 62:10) and your life and home become a worthy example and a testimony for others to emulate.

You will discover from the above that you are the one to profit when you submit to your husband. Receive grace for submission now in Jesus name!

Submit To Those In Authority!

Please be aware that even though your submission to your husband is primary, it is not only to your husband that submission is required; as a woman and as a minister's wife, the scripture says: *Obey them that have rule over you, and SUBMIT yourselves for they watch for your souls as they must give account. ...* (Hebrews 13:17). Also, *...submit yourselves to every ordinance of man for the lord's sake:* (2Peter. 2:13).

Apart from submitting to your husband, you are required to also submit to those in ruler ship and authority; as an act of submission to God Himself.

If your husband works under a ministry for instance, he has leaders over him and other ministers working under him. You must learn to submit to their authority and leadership too.

A Note of Warning

As this chapter closes, do take note of and be careful with this subtle stumbling block to submission; it is called 'pride.' One major cause of lack of submission is pride. It is an over-estimation of self. Pride is a killer weed; it kills seeds that have been sown.

Through obedience, the word and prayers; you can uproot any root or seed of pride in your life. I do not believe that one can be proud and not know it. As a minister's wife, pride will cause a bad spiritual odor to emanate from you to all that are around you and you can't live a fulfilled life that way.

Also, regular washing by the word of God to cleanse your heart against the planting of pride is necessary (Ephesians 5:26), because every act of pride births potential downfall (Proverbs 29: 23; 11:2).

Naturally, nobody enjoys a fall; so it is wise to heed the Lord's advice. "Pride leads to arguments; be humble, take advice and become wise (Proverbs 13: 10 TLB)." Give no room to pride! May the Lord guide your understanding.

FOOD FOR THOUGHT

"If you want to have peace in your home, you have to be willing to sacrifice your pride."

Joyce Meyer

Chapter 10

Qualities To Acquire

> ***For if these things be in you, and abound, they make you that ye shall*** **neither be** ***barren nor unfruitful in the knowledge of our Lord Jesus Christ.***
>
> 2 Peter 1:8

In order to fulfill the responsibilities already discussed, there are some qualities that are required. This however, is not an exhaustive list, but an understanding of these ones will definitely be helpful and enhance your effectiveness as a minister's wife.

Love

One of the primary qualities you must acquire so you can function effectively as a minister's wife is love. The scripture clearly declares: God is love!

> ***Beloved, let us love one another: for love is of God; and every one that loveth is born of God, and knoweth God.***

> ***He that loveth not knoweth not God; for God is love.***
>
> 1 John 4:7-8

As a born again child of God, you have this potential in you. Love is one of the seeds that was deposited in us at the point of salvation. You are born of the Spirit and that Spirit is the Spirit of God which is the Spirit of love.

Apart from having the nature of God to love, the Bible says:

> ***For God hath not given us the spirit of fear but of power, and of love and of a sound mind.***
>
> 2 Timothy 1: 7

All you need to do is to draw it out and make use of it. Stir it up. You are being Godly by loving.

As a minister's wife, you are required to live a life that radiates God's love. Love your children and husband; your' neighbors, in your local assembly and wherever you go. Your action speaks louder than your voice! The love of God in you must be expressed to those around you because love is not love until it is expressed.

Hatred must never be allowed in your life for whatever reason. When you arm yourself with the weapon of love, you find it easy to fulfill your responsibilities.

Love does cover a multitude of sin. Even when people offend you, as a minister's wife, correct them in love, forgive them and let it be a forgotten issue. Learn instant forgiveness and live a life of freedom.

Prayerfulness

You must be prayerful. The physical world is controlled by and from the spiritual world; and prayer is the means of linking the physical with the spiritual. The scripture says:

> ***While we look not at the things which are seen, but at the things which are not seen: for the things which are seen* are *temporal; but the things which are not seen* are *eternal.***
>
> 2 Corinthians 4:18

Those things which are not seen according to the above scripture can actually be seen and controlled in prayers.

The physical environment and atmosphere are actually greatly influenced by the spiritual. A good family atmosphere can be created through prayer. Therefore the power in prayer must not be downplayed .If you are weak in prayer you will soon stand in confusion. Prayer is the drug that prevents fainting:

> ***...men ought always to pray and not to faint,***
>
> Luke. 18:1

Praying 'always' does not necessarily indicate making request at all times, pacing up and down in your room always, nor being on your knees all day long. The scripture says:

> ***Praying always with all prayer and supplication in the Spirit, and watching thereunto with all perseverance and supplication for all saints;***
>
> Ephesians 6:18

Prayer is your link to God. An attitude of watchfulness, praise and worship to God is what it implies. You must maintain a spiritual atmosphere between God and you that makes for easy accessibility of either party at any time. You must learn the secret of Jesus' prayer life as related in the scripture:

> ***...in the morning rising up a great while before day, He went ... into a solitary place and ...prayed.***
>
> Mark. 1:35

Both privately and publicly, you must learn to sow seeds in prayer. The room of prayer is the room of power. A little time with God in prayer can change your destiny.

"No prayer, no fire; no power, no future," says Bishop David Oyedepo. There is a saying that a prayer-less Christian is a powerless Christian, and it is absolutely true. Quality time must be spent in the prayer room as a minister's wife. Time spent in the prayer room is never a waste, but an investment.

Spend Time to pray for your minister- husband, the family, the ministry and the work of the kingdom generally. Disallow complacency and nonchalance, which can stop you from reaching your God-given destiny. When you are prayerful, God supernaturally supplies power to you to be able to fulfill your responsibilities. This is because the prayer room is the power room of God. The power you need to fulfill your responsibilities will be released to you in prayer.

Dedication

Dedication is an important quality that you cannot do without if you must be effective. Without it, you cannot go far with God and with your calling. Dedication simply means to be committed to someone or something, giving yourself and services completely to it; to be sold out to it.

Dedication to God and commitment to your calling and that of your husband must be your priority as a minister's wife. Not much can be achieved in any area of life without dedication.

My husband once said: "Dedication is the mother of Distinction." This is very true. Every distinction is traceable to dedication. Whatever you are not dedicated to, you cannot be distinguished in.

Separate yourself from the things that can separate you from God. What is not worth dying for is not worth living for. Except you are totally committed to your call, you cannot be fruitful in it as a minister's wife. Concerning dedication, the scripture says:

> ***...Except a corn of wheat fall into the ground and die, it abideth alone.***
>
> John 12: 24

Apostle Paul, a man who is known for his dedication to his heavenly call said: *...for me to live is Christ and to die is gain...* (Galatians 2: 20.)

Dedication is it! For you to be distinguished, study the lives of other ministers' wives that have been and are being distinguished; you will discover that dedication is a major quality responsible for their distinction.

Dedication will produce the following in you: -

Diligence. Whatever you are dedicated to, you will be diligent about. Read this scripture on diligence with me:

> ***Wherefore the rather, brethren, give diligence to make your calling and election sure: for if ye do these things, ye shall never fall:***
>
> 2 Peter.1: 10

Diligence can be defined as steady effort, which leads to promotion. The Bible says:

> ***Seest thou a man diligent in his business? he shall stand before kings; he shall not stand before mean men.***
>
> Proverbs 22:29

Dreams cannot become reality outside of diligence. Distinction is a function of diligence. Even if it appears as if things are not happening as fast as you expected, keep at it and do not give up; as long as you are on the right track.

Hard work. Dedication will also produce hard work. When you are dedicated to a course, you work hard at it. You must be hard-working, if you are dedicated as a minister's wife. God's word says:

> ***...Not slothful in business...***
>
> Romans 12:11

You have no choice but to work hard, it is the trade mark of the dedicated. God does not condone laziness. You cannot afford to be lazy. He has spoken your greatness but He expects you to work hard by His spirit within you.

A lazy minister's wife does not have a future in the kingdom. You must work hard, at your own level so as to ensure that success in life and ministry becomes a practical reality. The scripture paints a picture of the virtuous woman in the book of Proverb, it says:

> ***...she eateth not the bread of idleness...***
>
> Proverbs 31:27

Don't be caught idling around when you should be busy praying, studying, evangelizing, counseling or doing whatever you have been assigned to do.

When you are truly dedicated, the two virtues above will have a free course in your life.

Faithfulness

This is another quality that you must acquire for you to be effective. You have to be faithful as a minister's wife. There is a call to faithfulness in scriptures; until you are faithful in a little, God will not commit more to your hands. The word says:

> ***It is required in a steward that a man be found faithful.***
>
> 1 Corinthians 4: 2

Faithfulness does not necessarily mean skill, or anointing. For instance, you don't have to head the prayer unit of the ministry or the believers' class; head the bible study group, have miracles take place through your hands or minister all over the world before you can be faithful.

Faithfulness means doing what you are expected to do correctly without supervision. Some people, especially women would only do what is expected when people who will command them are around. That is 'face fullness' (eye-service) and not faithfulness. Read what the word says here:

> ***Who then is that faithful and wise steward, whom his Lord shall make ruler over his household, to give them their portion or meat in due season? Blessed is that servant, whom his Lord WHEN HE COMETH SHALL FIND SO DOING!***
>
> Luke. 12:42

Only the faithful will be rewarded not the 'face-full!' Faithfulness is like a driving force that enables you fulfill your responsibilities as a minister's wife, with ease.

The future of the faithful is guaranteed and his rising unlimited. And I am talking about faithfulness both to God and to men. How faithful are you? Until you're faithful in a little, the future of the much you desire can never become a reality.

Sound relationships

Relationship begins with your manner of approach. To build a good relationship, you must be approachable;

not moody or tight faced. Let people know you for your warm and welcoming nature.

You must be able to relate easily, quickly and in a charming manner with others. Abigail would not have won the love of David but for her good countenance. The Bible says:

> ***Now the name of the man* was *Nabal; and the name of his wife Abigail: and* she was *a woman of good understanding, and of a beautiful countenance...***
>
> 1 Samuel 25:3

Your relationships will not go well if all you focus on are wrong perceptions and negative surmising. Moodiness destroys relationships; long 'facedness' makes you unattractive while also misrepresenting your person.

Remember that you cannot do without people. Ministry itself is all about impacting peoples' lives positively.

You must be slow to wrath (James 1:19). Do not be easily offended, but be forgiving. Here, love has a part to play because as you stir it up *"love covers a multitude of sin"* (1 Peter. 4:8). Even when you are justified to be upset due to a wrong committed against you, the word of God is a sure anchor, it says:

> ***Great peace have they, which love thy law and***

nothing shall offend them

Psalms 119:165

If you must rebuke someone, it must be done in love.

There may be some relationships, however, that you may need to refrain from in order to maintain godly peace. In such cases, your love for God and His word will shelter you from the effects of any harm from such relationships.

However, you must have pure motives for every relationship you are in. The Bible says:

> ***...the end of the commandment is charity out of a pure heart, and of a good conscience and of faith unfeigned.***
>
> 1 Timothy 1: 5

When your relationship with people is healthy, you will find it easy to fulfill your responsibilities as a minister's wife.

Servant hood

This is one major quality that every minister's wife who desires success must possess. Servant hood is possessing wholehearted readiness to be of service to God and His kingdom.

Servant hood can be likened to the rope with which God lifts you from a low position to a high one. Your lifting will meet you at the point of service because in God's kingdom, promotion does not jump on people; it comes via active service.

Zechariah was in active service in the temple, despite the fact that he and his wife were well stricken in age and childless (Luke 1:5-14). But the faithful God visited them right where he was serving; angel Gabriel gave him the message from God. The scripture records:

> ***...thy wife Elizabeth shall bear thee a son... thou shalt have joy and gladness...***
>
> Luke 1: 13-14

If you have a heart for the welfare of God's kingdom, God's heart will be loaded with blessings for you.

Woman, you must identify a specific place where you fit in and faithfully serve God there. Do not be either a bench- warmer or a title- carrier; be in service. God rewards service, not church attendance or title. Be service conscious.

Zechariah, in Luke 1:5-14 received an angelic visitation as he served God. Angels relate better with believers who are in service as God's servants because they (angels) are also servants.

Remember the saying: birds of the same feather flock together. Angels met him where he was placed. Service distinguished Zechariah; it will do the same for you.

As you serve God as a minister's wife, expect angelic visitation also.

Your 'but' shall be taken away as you faithfully serve God. Barrenness was the "but" in Zechariah's life and it was taken away as he served God. Disallow pressures, needs, concerns, and the likes, to press you out.

Let nothing separate you from God and your service to Him and to his kingdom. Stop struggling for placement; serve your way to placement! Be persistent in your service; remember that continuity is the rule of the game. Locate where you rightfully belong and serve God there with the whole of your heart.

With these qualities in place in your life, you are on your way to distinction as a minister's wife. Please be aware, these qualities don't jump on people, they are acquired.

So, if any of these is missing in your life, you must take practical steps to work on yourself until they are formed in you. How then, do I acquire these qualities? You may ask. Come along with me and let's see how.

How to Acquire These Qualities

God, who knew you would be a minister's wife, has already made provision for how you can acquire these qualities. Here are some of the avenues for acquiring them:

Asking

If you require any of these qualities, the first thing you need to do is to ask from God. Jesus said: *"He that asketh, recieveth"* (Matthew 7:8) God is the giver. He will not withhold any good thing from you (Proverbs 3:27). How do you ask? You ask in prayer.

Through prayer, you make your request known to God. Ask and believe you have received, nothing wavering; and you will receive the enabling to exhibit these qualities.

God will not deny you, if you require it and ask Him; in faith and sincerity of your heart. Everyone that 'asketh', 'receiveth'; that includes you. Whatever good quality you see in a minister's wife, you can ask the same from God in prayer and God will not deny you; for:

> ***...no good thing will He withhold from them that walk uprightly***
>
> Psalms 84:11

God is no respecter of persons (Romans 2:11). Stop wishing, ask God for any of those qualities that you require to function effectively as a minister's wife and He will give it to you liberally.

Association

The association you keep either makes or breaks you; it doesn't leave you the same. Relationships either add to you or take away from you. You are a reflection of the company you keep. There are certain traits that rub off on you when you relate closely with someone. The scripture says:

> ***Make no friendship with an angry; and with a furious man thou shalt not go: lest thou LEARN HIS WAYs and get a snare to thy soul***
>
> Proverbs 22:24-25

Here, it shows that some things – qualities, character traits can be cultivated through friendships and associations.

The bible also says: *He that WALKETH with WISE MEN shall be WISE...* (Proverbs 13:20.) You do not need to be a fool to be destroyed; you only need to keep company with a fool and you can't escape destruction.

From the above scripture, it is evident that you as a minister's wife should look out for useful, meaningful associations through which you can acquire the qualities that you desire. The relationship of Elijah and Elisha clearly demonstrates that Elisha's association with Elijah was one cardinal reason why he was able to operate in Elijah's anointing.

Therefore, you as a minister's wife should look for and relate closely with another minister's wife, preferably one that is spiritually higher or more experienced than you; who possesses the qualities you desire to have, so that virtue can flow to you.

A wise man once said: "You will be what you are today in five (5) years time except for the books you read and the company you keep." There is a saying in this part of the world that: "Show me your friend and I will tell you who you are."

By and large, the associations you keep go a long way in determining who you are and how far you will ever go in life. If your friend is lazy, in all probability you will be lazy too. If the friend you keep is covetous and nags, you also will automatically learn her ways for: *two cannot walk together except they be agreed* (Amos 3:3). Keep the right association and tap into the grace for greater effectiveness.

Hard Core Study

One major way to acquire the qualities you require for effectiveness is through dedicated word study. The Bible says: *thou through thy commandments have made me wiser than mine enemies...* (Psalms 119:98). Through the word and study of biblical examples, your mind becomes renewed to think and act in whatever fashion the word dictates; whether it is in area of faithfulness, love, diligence, etc. This is why the Bible says:

> ***Study to show yourself approved unto God, a workman that needeth not to be ashamed rightly dividing the word of truth***
>
> 2 Timothy 2: 15

As you study, the ability to rightly divide the word and take right actions is imparted. If you are ignorant in the word, and are not studious as a minister's wife; you will not be able to dig out the gems you need from the word of God.

You must be married afresh to the word of God, daily. Quality time must be spent in the study of the word; learn to bend down and study, discipline yourself to burn the midnight candle until those qualities are imparted.

Whatever quality is imparted via the word of God will definitely last and stand the test of time. For every challenge you face in life as a minister's wife, the answer is in the deep (the word). The scripture states:

> ***For you shall know the truth and the truth shall set you free***
>
> John 8:32

Obviously, your depth in the word determines your height in life and ministry. How long you have been a minister's wife is not as important as how much depth you have. Don't assume that you know the word, so you don't end up in frustration.

Program yourself for a lifestyle of continuous fatness in the word. There is no non-studious minister's wife that has a future in this kingdom. Insight produces foresight and foresight is the pacesetter for accomplishment. Get fed to a point where you can overflow to others and feed them as well.

The Holy Spirit

The Holy Spirit is the power of God, your enabler; without Him, all your efforts to acquire these qualities will be in vain. Concerning this, the scripture says:

> ***But ye shall receive power after that the Holy Ghost is come upon you...***
>
> Acts 1:8

To be able to exhibit these qualities, you need the power of the Holy Spirit. Power is defined as the ability to do work. For you to get the ability that is required to exhibit these qualities, you need the power of the Holy Spirit. The Holy Spirit is your enabler and energizer.

Every minister's wife needs to be baptized in the Holy Spirit with the evidence of speaking in tongues, irrespective of your denomination. The Holy Spirit is the gift of God to every believer. You can be baptized by asking Jesus Christ – the baptizer to baptize you in the Holy Spirit. John the Baptist said concerning Jesus is:

> ***John answered, saying unto them all, I indeed baptize you with water; but one mightier than I cometh, the latchet of whose shoes I am not worthy to unloose: he shall baptize you with the Holy Ghost and with fire:***
>
> Luke 3:16

If you require assistance in this area, feel free to contact me through the address behind this book.

To make any impact in the ministry to which God has called you, you require the help of the Holy Spirit. It is the Holy Spirit that gives you understanding of the word of God; He guides you into all truth (John 16:13), via the word. This explains why the Bible says:

> ***...for it is God which worketh in you both to will and to do of His good pleasure***
>
> Philippians 2: 13

Without the power of the Holy Spirit, you will be unable to put on these qualities, even though you know them. But when you are baptized in the Holy Spirit, you constantly put on spiritual energy by speaking in tongues and getting yourself built up so as to put these qualities to work. The Bible says:

But ye beloved building up yourselves on your most holy faith, praying in the Holy Ghost

Jude verse 20

The more you speak in unknown tongues, the more energized your spirit becomes and the easier it is for you to exhibit the qualities that you desire. You must remember that you are powerless without the Holy Ghost power. You must be baptized in the Holy Spirit.

FOOD FOR THOUGHT

Whatever you would make habitual, practice it...

Epictetus

Chapter 11

The Place Of Fellowship

Then Daniel went to his house, and made the thing known to Hananiah, Mishael, and Azariah, his companions:

That they would desire mercies of the God of heaven concerning this secret; that Daniel and his fellows should not perish with the rest of the wise* men *of Babylon.

Daniel 2:17-18

There is a place for fellowship with people of the same calling; apart from your involvement in various programmes, ministry affairs and the like. You can never out grow fellowship with your companions.

The *Oxford Advanced Learner's Dictionary* defines the word 'fellowship" as "a friendly association with others; companionship, a group or society of people sharing a common interest." As privileged ministers' wives, fellowship and friendly association with fellow ministers' wives is of utmost importance and cannot be over-emphasized because you share a common interest with them.

Remember the saying: "water seeks its own level." There are situations, circumstances and challenges of life that are peculiar to ministers' wives only. When such challenges are shared with other ministers' wives, it becomes easy to handle them maturely. This is the essence of such fellowships.

Interestingly, the word 'fellowship' is made up of two separate words: 'fellow' and 'ship'. This in essence can be interpreted to mean fellows in the same ship. You are in the ministry 'ship' with fellow ministers' wives. It is your responsibility to maximize this opportunity and privilege rather than taking things for granted.

Daniel in the above scripture went back to his friends who were his companions, the people who understood and had the same belief with him; to share the challenge at hand.

Thank God he had a place of fellowship to resort to at such a time. As companions, they prayed and the dream of the king was revealed. Miraculously, they overcame! There is power in fellowship, especially with others in the same company with you. This explains why the scripture says:

Iron sharpeneth iron; so a man sharpeneth the

countenance of his friend.

Proverbs 27:17

Iron is a piece of metal synonymous with strength. When it comes in contact with another piece of iron during sharpening, its strength is made manifest by the sparks of fire released. The advantage of this contact is that it leads to increased strength and usefulness of the iron, and thereby guarantees speed in accomplishing tasks.

However, worthy of note is the fact that until it comes in contact with another piece of iron for sharpening, its strength cannot be made manifest. It is therefore possible for its potential strength to remain blunt and not be productively engaged, for lack of necessary contact.

Every Christian can be likened to a piece of individual iron. So, as a minister's wife, you have been endowed with some measure of strength by God; potentially. However, there is a limit to which that potential strength can be made manifest without contact with other pieces of iron-Christians. That explains the reason and importance of the place of fellowship in the life of the believer generally and the minister's wife in particular.

For a minister's wife, there are times when what you are confronted with or going through may seem peculiar only to you, but by the time you share fellowship with others in "your own company", you may discover that you are not alone in such situations (1 Corinthians 10: 13); you are encouraged and are therefore able to forge ahead in the face of such challenges.

The Apostles are an example to follow, they constantly returned to their own company to receive strength in their days. The Bible gave an account of what happened after they were threatened by the council

> ***And being let go, they went to their own company and reported all that the chief priests and elders had said unto them.***
>
> ***And when they had prayed, the place was shaken where they were assembled together; and they were all filled with the Holy Ghost and they spake the word of God with boldness.***
>
> Acts 4:23, 31

In the early church, the disciples had their own company that they resorted to continually. As a ministers' wife, you must also be able to locate and enjoy fellowship with others in your own company; where related issues can be handled, prayers prayed together and fellowship shared.

If the disciples in the early church did that, then this end time, it is of utmost importance to identify your own company and resort to it. The scripture says:

> ***... one chase a thousand, and two put ten thousand to flight ...***
>
> Deuteronomy 32: 30

The above scripture becomes practically possible through healthy, constant and effective fellowship.

Attend seminars, workshops, meetings and gatherings of fellow ministers' wives where others can sharpen your life for the better. Personally, whenever I attend Christian gatherings, conventions and seminars; I always look forward to a time of meeting with other ministers' wives: that's my company!

Fellowshipping with your fellow minister's wives shows that you are obedient to the word of God, and by so doing you command the blessings of obedience (Isaiah 1: 19 -20). The scriptures exhort us, it says:

> ***Not forsaking the assembling of ourselves together, as the manner of some* is; *but exhorting* one another: *and so much the more, as ye see the day approaching.***
>
> Hebrews 10:25

Never under-estimate the virtues, values and benefits of sharing fellowship with fellow ministers wives, women in your own company! Never be tempted to forsake it- it's for you benefit and up-liftment! Obedience to God's word always brings reward.

What are the benefits of fellowshipping with your company? Let us examine some of them briefly here.

Increased knowledge and exploits

The Good News bible translation of Proverbs 27:17 says: *People learn from one another....* When you are in fellowship with others you become more knowledgeable of your new position in Christ and your responsibilities as a minister's wife.

There is an impartation of knowledge by virtue of rubbing your mind with that of other ministers' wives. You learn new things. This new knowledge makes for greater strength, and so your strength is increased.

Knowledge is synonymous with strength. From the bible, we understand that:

> ***A wise man is strong; yea, a man of knowledge increaseth strength.***
>
> Proverbs 24:5

How strong you are determines how much exploits you do in life. *...But the people that do KNOW their God shall be strong and do exploits.* (Daniel 11:32). There is a limit to how much exploits you can do in life without adequate relevant knowledge. There is therefore a need to seek knowledge and pursue it.

When you come in contact with such people, you discover there are people who have successfully trodden the path you are on; you may discover that there are those who have faced greater challenges than you and have succeeded. That strengthens, encourages and energises you to keep on; knowing fully well that you'll also overcome.

Wise counsel and speedy accomplishments

What better group is there to receive wise counsel on various issues related to minister's wives than your own company? It is easy to receive practical counsel from someone who has gone through what you are experiencing. The bible recognizes the place of wise counsel, it says:

> ***Where no counsel* is, *the people fall: but in the multitude of counselors* there is *safety.***
>
> Proverbs 11: 14

Costly mistakes can be avoided; this enhances your speed in life and ministry. You can conduct expository studies, share ideas, ask questions and rub minds together during such meetings. Remember that for you to see farther; you need to stand on the shoulders of those that have gone ahead of you.

Exercise and profiting of gifts and talents

Exercise of gifts and talents is another benefit that fellowshipping with other minister' wives affords you, this in turns bring about great profiting. Some ministers' wives are endowed in one area or the other with the grace and ability to exhort and stir up others. However, the scripture says you should ... *grow in (this) grace...* (2 Peter 3: 18); and it is only *...by reason of use* (Hebrews 5:14) that such grace can grow.

Thus, such forums create opportunity to exercise the grace of God upon your life and then it is exceedingly multiplied. Whatever gift or talent you do not put to work (good use) cannot yield profit. The purpose of your gifts and talents is to bring profit, the Bible says:

> ***But the manifestation of the Spirit is given to every man to profit withal.***
>
> 1 Corinthians 12:7

When you become aware of what fellow ministers' wives are doing with the grace of God upon their lives, their exploits and various contributions to the kingdom of God at various levels; it awakens, motivates and challenges you to a life of greater productivity in the kingdom.

You must however be careful and ensure you are not caught in the snare of comparison and competition

(2 Corinthians 10: 12). Never be found competing with or trying to "out-do" one another, it is not wisdom; but rather complementing and learning from one another.

Boldness

Boldness is required if you must be effective as a minister's wife. You can never achieve much without it. Boldness is strength of heart and it can be obtained when you fellowship with fellow ministers' wives. Whenever the apostles returned to their company after having prayed, they usually became bolder.

> ***And when they had prayed, the place was shaken … they were assembled TOGETHER … and they spake the word of God with BOLDNESS***
>
> Acts 5:31

As you share fellowship with fellow ministers' wives, boldness which is the winners' trade secret is imparted. You can never amount to much nor command exploits in ministry without boldness, at whatever level!

These, among others are the things you stand to gain as you fellowship with fellow ministers' wives.

By now, perhaps you are wondering how it could be possible for you to be in all such gatherings, meetings and seminars of ministers' wives in the name of fellowshipping with others; especially with your every day busy schedule.

Aside, there may be those you would have loved to share fellowship with but are not physically within your reach or are far away from you.

The good news is: even though physically fellowshipping with others is the primary and most preferred and recommended means, and you should do all you can to get involved; there are other ways whereby you can fellowship without necessarily being around in person.

However, please be aware that these other means are no substitutes for physically attending profitable gatherings of other ministers' wives; rather, they should be additions. These other means of fellowship include but are not limited to the following:

Through the printed page – read books and other written materials

Read books and other written materials by or about other ministers' wives. The printed page is one major means of fellowship that is readily available for you to enjoy at anytime.

There are people that you may never have the privilege of coming in contact with face-to-face, but you can always tap into the grace of God upon their lives through the printed page.

For instance: up till the time of writing this book, I have not been privileged to meet Mama Dodie Osteen one-on-one; but her book titled "Healed of Cancer" is one of the books that inspired me during my 'journey through the valley of the shadow of death' when the devil attacked my body, as documented in one of my books titled "Rescued From Destruction".

Every minister's wife should cultivate a reading culture. The Bible says:

> ***Till I come, give attendance to reading...***
>
> 1 Timothy 4:13

It is God's command and all His commands have benefits. Daniel received understanding from books *...I Daniel understood by books ...* (Daniel 9:2). The scripture tells us as believers that we should get understanding *...with all thy getting get understanding.* (Proverbs 4:7). A good understanding of any subject gives you favor in that area (Proverbs13: 15).

As you read books and other materials written by and about ministers' wives especially those who have done what you are trying to do, your understanding of your office is deepened and favor graces your path in all you do. Don't claim to be so busy that you do not have time for reading. Create time for it out of your busy schedule and you will be amazed how much you can be blessed by this.

You must however be very cautious and selective in your choice of books. Choose books, magazines and other written materials that are relevant to your specific areas of need and written by proven authors; someone who has something extra to offer and to add, with proofs.

This is very crucial especially because whenever you read a material, the spirit of the author also rubs off on you; so you must be careful and selective.

Through the electronic media - Listen to their messages

Bless God for the advancement of technology that we enjoy these days; you can listen to messages (audio and video) of other ministers' wives, especially those who are ahead of you in ministry.

The electronic media is a readily available means of fellowship for you to easily enjoy; anytime, anywhere! As you do this, there is transference of graces and impartation of unction by the Holy Spirit. The scripture says:

> ***And the spirit entered into me when he SPAKE unto me, and set me upon my feet, that I heard him that spake unto me.***
>
> Ezekiel 2:2, 3:24

Your spirit man will be strengthened; the spirit of your mind (Ephesians 4:23) will be tremendously renewed. Anything you hear or see on a regular basis becomes consciously and subconsciously a part of you. You are what you continually behold. You will just begin to walk in line with it.

Keys To Healthy Fellowship

In order to receive maximum benefit and fulfillment from fellowship with one another as women of the same company, some key factors should be taken note of. Let's examine some of them briefly here.

Esteeming others better than yourself

Never think or carry a 'better-than-thou' mentality or attitude in relating with others, else it will affect how beneficial the fellowship can be to you. This mentality injures the spirit of love and the flow of the Spirit. The Bible says:

> ***Let nothing be done through strife ...but in lowliness of mind let each esteem other better than themselves...***
>
> Philippians 2:4

The above scripture enjoins each to esteem others better than themselves, each person should possess the meekness required to learn from one another; because there is always something to learn even from those who appear to be of a lower spiritual standing than yours.

Some 'highly placed' or 'senior' ministers' wives feel that to be in a fellowship with another minister's wife whose husband is not as 'anointed', popular, or well known as her husband is a demotion. This is an attitude that kills fellowship. Besides, you cannot learn or gain anything that way. The scripture says:

> ***Nay, much more those members of the body, which seem to be more feeble are necessary:***
>
> ***And those members of the body, which we think to be less honourable, upon these we bestow more abundant honour; and our uncomely parts have more abundant comeliness***
>
> ***... but God hath tempered the body together having given more abundant honour to that part which lacked:***
>
> ***That there should be no schism in the body but... the same care for one another.***
>
> 1 Corinthians 12: 22-25

When Naaman the leper heard the word of Prophet Elisha, he felt he would be stooping too low to go bathe in the river Jordan as the prophet commanded (2 Kings 5: 1-14). However, his deliverance lay right there; and thank God he listened to his servant who encouraged him to obey the prophet, and he got healed.

When you have to relate with those who are "junior" to you, don't despise it because you never know how much blessing awaits you by so doing!

To come to 'your company' is to receive spiritual, mental, social, and physical refreshing, whether they are older or younger, senior or junior to you.

Take a look at this: each part of the human body has something profitable to offer, no matter how small. There should be the consciousness that you possess an ability or grace, which is meant to be shared with others.

There are those who look up to you and need your knowledge, experiences and grace to enable them get to their God-ordained destination. It would amount to selfishness and wickedness to deliberately withdraw from fellowship when you know God has endowed you with something that others need.

You are not insignificant, no matter who you are or are not involved with. There is something within that can be offered to young and old, senior or junior. The scriptures encourage us in this truth when it says,

> ***...and so become more and more in every way like Christ who is the head of his body, the church.***
>
> ***Under his direction, the whole body is fitted together***

> ***perfectly and each part in its own special way HELPS the other parts, so that the whole body is HEALTHY and growing and full of love***
>
> Ephesians 4:15-16 TLB

Each part of the body has something to supply to others. With this consciousness, there can be a healthy flow of love and insight during fellowship.

Be open and ready to receive

You need to be open-minded before you can receive or benefit from any such fellowship. Expect and look forward to being blessed by and in such meetings. This is very crucial because your expectation defines and sets the boundaries for your life.

What you expect determines what you get. If you expect nothing, you get nothing! Never see such meetings as a societal gathering, but a spiritual service station. In actual fact, God always meets us at the level of our expectation! This explains why the scripture says:

> ***... thine expectation shall not be cut off.***
>
> Proverbs 23:18; 24:14

It is your expectation and openness that sets the pace for your experiences in such fellowship meetings. Until you are open and receptive, the grace of God upon them can never flow in your direction nor benefit you.

So, never look down on anyone in those meetings; rather see each one as having something to offer, and be receptive when others stand to share.

Avoid gossip and busy-bodying

In other to have a healthy and successful fellowship, avoid busy-bodying. Fellowship is not a place for gossiping, backbiting or discussing other women's matters.

The scriptures, speaking concerning certain women seriously warns against this:

> ***Having damnation, because they have cast off their first faith.***
>
> ***And withal they learn to be idle, wandering about from house to house; and not only idle, but tattlers also and busy- bodies, speaking things which they out not.***
>
> 1 Timothy 5: 12-13

Beware; busy-bodying leads to damnation and can make you lose your first love for God. To engage in gossip and busy-bodying is to walk disorderly (2 Thessalonians 3:11), such people end up suffering for it (1 Peter 4:15); you will not suffer!

Let your coming together be to share, sharpen and improve one another; for better performance. The Bible says:

And above all things have fervent charity among yourselves: for charity shall cover the multitude of sins.

1 Peter 4:8

Such meetings should not be a place where you strip others naked, especially in their absence; more so if it is in a bid to cover up your own inadequacies.

We are to see Christ's nature grow and manifest in each other more and more, not the devil's nature.

Set your priorities right

Do not allow fellowshipping with others to be an excuse to neglect your personal relationship with God, neglect your calling, family, business, or priority matters. The scripture says:

...study to be quiet and to do your own business...

1 Thessalonians 4:11

There are those who attend every kind of fellowship at the expense of putting their lives and homes in order. There are others too, who are inactive in spiritual things; claiming it is because they have to keep the home. This is unhealthy and can hinder growth. Here, balance is the key; avoid both extremes. Remember: **Iron sharpens iron!**

Wisdom will provide the right balance, so that as a

minister's wife you are found faithful in all your responsibilities and in your fellowship with your company.

Expectedly, such fellowships should feature sessions of praise, prayer, testimonies, word sharing, interaction with one another and the like. "One tree never makes a forest", says an adage. When you fellowship with women of like minds and calling, life and ministry becomes more meaningful and fulfilling for you.

FOOD FOR THOUGHT

You cannot see Him (God), without men longing to see you.

Faith Oyedepo

Chapter 12

Don't Die In Silence!

...but woe to him that is alone when he falleth; for he hath not another to help him up

Ecclesiastes 4:10

Many are victims of their present predicament just because they kept mute. It is not as if there is no help around but they refused to call for one. May be they do not want others to know or they feel that without their talking, people around should understand, know and attend to their needs.

Silence is defined to be the absence of sound. You cannot successfully pass any message across without making sound of some sort.

Even the dumb call your attention by making sound of certain sort, they communicate! That means you cannot successfully pass across any message in silence. If at all there is any message being passed across, such a message can be misinterpreted and misunderstood.

It is therefore important for you to make sound that can be understood.

Many minister's wives are not left out as they suffer in silence, live unfulfilled lives and are frustrated. Many things are going wrong on the home front and in the ministry, yet they keep numb; never seeking help or godly counsel.

Unfortunately, in process of time, many resort to and become addicted to drugs, food, pornography, and alcohol and such other things that they feel will help them out of their predicament.

Then one day after months or years of "hiding" from the truth, something terrible happens-divorce, a police case, adultery, the disintegration or collapse of a ministry and so on. This ought not to be so.

There is no man on earth that can read what is in your mind or what you are going through, that is why you have to open up so you don't die in silence!

Only God is the Omniscience, the all knowing. Even with this attribute, He still demands that we open our mouth and ask. The Bible says:

> ***Ask, and it shall be given you; seek, and ye shall find; knock, and it shall be opened unto you:***
>
> Matthew 7:7

Why will you die in silence when there is help around

you? From this chapter you will learn some tips that will help you come out of your cocoon and seek for help when it is needed.

Why then do many refuse to call for help?

Let us examine some of the reasons for this here.

Pride

You need to understand what the Bible says in the book of Ecclesiastes 1: 9(c)... *and there is no new thing under the sun.*

Whatever might be your calling or assignment, somebody somewhere has done something like it before. There is also somebody somewhere doing something similar to it right now. They have experienced or are experiencing whatever you are being confronted with right now. They have confronted and slain the giants you are dealing with. It is wisdom to connect and learn from such people.

Calling for help when you need it is not a sign of weakness, rather; it is wisdom! So, do not give room to pride by refusing to seek godly counsel.

Pride in most cases is the reason why many people do not seek for help when it is most needed. Pride is a destroyer; it has destroyed many great destinies, don't let it destroy yours!

The Bible categorically says:

> ***Pride goeth before destruction, and an haughty spirit before a fall.***
>
> Proverbs 16: 18

Do not let the devil deceive you to make you think that you are so 'anointed' and therefore you can handle all challenges yourself. Nothing can be farther from the truth!

Open up and ventilate your life for greater productivity and effectiveness!

The Bible says one shall chase a thousand and two shall put ten thousand to flight (Deuteronomy 32:30). What you are passing through might be more than what you alone can 'chase'. It is not a shameful thing to open up to those who can be of help.

Making Excuses

Making excuses for things that are going wrong is another reason why many suffer in silence.

Jesus told a parable how a certain man made a great supper, and invited many to come. Despite the fact that all things were ready, they all made excuses and did not attend. The Bible says:

> ***And they all with one consent began to make excuse.***
> Luke 14: 18

The master of the house was angry with them and brought in others to take their place; due to excuses. Your place in destiny shall not be taken by another!

Abigail is an example of a wise woman as recorded in the Bible (1 Samuel 25:14-28). She could have used her husband's foolishness as an excuse not to be liberal and that would have resulted to blood birth in her home. Instead, she opened up:

> ***Let not my lord, I pray thee, regard this man of Belial,* even *Nabal: for as his name* is, so is *he; Nabal* is *his name, and folly* is *with him: but I thine handmaid saw not the young men of my lord, whom thou didst send.***
>
> ***Now therefore, my lord,* as *the LORD liveth, and* as *thy soul liveth, seeing the LORD hath withheld thee from coming to* shed *blood, and from avenging thyself with thine own hand, now let thine enemies, and they that seek evil to my lord, be as Nabal.***
> 1 Samuel 25:25-26

Stop making excuses for things that are going wrong, having every reason in the world and explanation why things are not the way they should be. Instead, be a woman of wisdom; take action, make a move and seek help.

Pretence

Pretence is behaving in a way that is intended to deceive people. Pretence is what the bible calls hypocrisy. Jesus was always against hypocrites. Speaking about this, the Bible says:

> ***unto you, scribes and Pharisees, hypocrites! For ye make clean the outside of the cup and of the platter, but within Woe they are full of extortion and excess.***
>
> Matthew 23: 25

Stop covering up! Do not pretend that things are going on the right way when you know it is not. Who are you deceiving? Do you want to live in deceit all your life?

Stop consoling yourself with the fact that it is so with everybody! You'll be surprised that you are the only one left, still caught in the web of pretence; others have left! Wake up and begin to take action. Be open and sincere with yourself.

Pretence is costlier than you think. When you pretend, you make a fool of yourself. In actual fact the person you are trying to impress through pretense might know you more than you think.

When Jesus met that Samaritan woman beside the well she appeared to be religious and she wanted to make Jesus feel that all was well with her (John 4: 4-18). But one revealing question from Jesus broke down her wall of pretence.

The Bible says:

> ***Jesus saith unto her, Go, call thy husband, and come hither***
>
> John 4:16

Do not wait until your balloon of pretence is punctured. Sit down and write those areas where you know that you need help and prayerfully begin to take action.

Are you being faced with loneliness, or you feel you are not giving your children adequate attention? May be your problem is finances or it has to do with ill health, don't keep it to yourself. There is no wisdom in dying in silence. Open up and give more meaning to your life.

Ignorance

This is lack of knowledge, understanding or information about something. It is one other major reason why many minister's wives keep to themselves, dying inside! Little wonder then, the Bible says:

> ***My people are destroyed for lack of knowledge: because thou hast rejected knowledge, I will also reject thee, that thou shalt be no priest to me: seeing***

thou hast forgotten the law of thy God, I will also forget thy children.

Hosea 4: 6

To be destroyed in this context means to be robbed of honor and dignity. For you not to be robbed of dignity and honor as a minister's wife, you must shun ignorance and go for knowledge.

The truth that you know is the one that can make you free! This explains why the scripture says:

And ye shall know the truth, and the truth shall make you free.

John 8: 32

Remember: "what you don't know may be what is killing you." Inadequate information about a particular situation can pose a problem. Uzzah's death in 2 Samuel 6:7 could be as a result of ignorance. Perhaps he was not adequately informed that no one should touch the ark of God but he did and was punished.

And the anger of the LORD was kindled against Uzzah; and God smote him there for **his** ***error; and there he died by the ark of God.***

After this incidence, the ark was properly carried and they were all blessed. You will not be a 'scape goat' for others to learn from. Crave for knowledge, be adequately informed, and do not die in silence through ignorance.

Laziness

This is another reason why some keep mute rather than open up, until they die in silence. A lazy person is slow, too relaxed, not willing to work and put effort into anything; therefore he is prone to all manners of harassment. The Bible says:

> ***Not slothful in business; fervent in spirit; serving the Lord;***
>
> Romans 12:11

Many minister's wives are so lazy at so many things. Lazy in prayer; reading books; reading the bible, and even in relating to other senior ministers. Wake up from your slumber and begin to put more effort into life so it can deliver its best to you!

Read with me this most revealing episode about the field of the slothful in the Bible:

> ***I went by the field of the slothful, and by the vineyard of the man void of understanding;***
>
> ***And, lo, it was all grow over with thorns, and nettles had covered the face thereof, and the stone wall thereof was broken down.***
>
> ***Then I saw, and considered it well: I looked upon***

it, and received instruction.

Yet a little sleep, a little slumber, a little folding of the hands to sleep:

So shall thy poverty come as one that traveleth; and thy want as an armed man.

Proverbs 24: 30-34

The slothful is void of understanding and will end up in poverty!

Laziness manifests in procrastination. I will do it later, next week; before long, a year is gone and the situation still remains. Deal with procrastination; this is what graduates to laziness.

Insensitivity

Many minister's wives are not aware of what is going on around them; they refuse to give importance to happenings. They are spiritually asleep.

Spiritual insensitivity is the undoing of many. The Bible says:

Wherefore he saith, awake thou that sleepest, and arise from the desd, and Christ shall give thee light.

Ephesians 5: 14

A lot of things happen per time, so seek fresh encounters with God. Seek for fresh anointing per day, update yourself and seek progress, continuously.

Remember the word of God says:

> ***See then that ye walk circumspectly, not as fools, but as wise, Redeeming the time, because the days are evil.***
>
> Ephesians 5:15-16

God's faithfulness is great and they are new every morning (Lamentations 3: 23)!

Stubbornness

Surprisingly, some minister's wives actually know that they need help in certain areas, they also know how to call for help; but they just would not, due to stubbornness.

The biblical truth on this subject comes very clear, it states:

> ***For rebellion* is as *the sin of witchcraft, and stubbornness* is as *iniquity and idolatry. Because thou hast rejected the word of the LORD, he hath also rejected thee from being king.***
>
> 1 Samuel 15:23

Stubbornness and idolatry are rated equally, scripturally. It is a terrible sin, it makes God reject you; it ultimately destroys! Shouldn't you run from it? You shall not be destroyed via stubbornness in Jesus name.

King Saul knew he sinned against God and needed

help but he did not call for it, may be because he wanted to keep his reputation before men. He turned deaf ear to divine instruction and he lost his throne as king.

Frustration

Some minister's wives do not call for help even when they know they need one due to frustration. Their past efforts and plans seem not to have been able to achieve their desired goals. They have tried all they seem to know but it is not working. So, they are reluctant to seek any further help.

Please bear in mind the fact that there is no situation that is hopeless. Naman, the centurion leper had sought for various helps but the leprosy remained. When he finally got to the place of help in Israel, he almost missed it as a result of frustration.

He said :

> ***...Behold, I thought, He will surely come out to me, and stand, and call on the name of the LORD his God, and strike his hand over the place, and recover the leper.***
>
> ***Are not Abana and Pharpar, rivers of Damascus, better than all the waters of Israel? May I not wash in them, and be clean? So he turned and went away in a rage.***
>
> 2 Kings 5:11-12

But thank God for his servant who told him:

> ***...My father,* if *the prophet had bid thee* do some *great thing, wouldest thou not have done* it*? how much rather then, when he saith to thee, Wash, and be clean?***
>
> 2 Kings 5:13

Usually, the enemy brings frustration when you are closest to your help. You will not be frustrated out of your help zone in Jesus name.

Insecurity

Some do not call for help because they do not feel safe or protected. They are afraid of being disappointed. That you have experienced some disappointment in some persons in time past does not mean that everyone will let you down, not keeping your secret.

Do not let this stronghold rob you of your desired and much needed help. Do not be intimidated about what people might say if you open up to them and they get to know you more intimately. What you need is solutions to your situation; in as much as you get it, you are safe.

Having examined why some minister's wives refuse to call for help, let us look at how to overcome challenges so as not to die in silence.

The Way Out

> ***There hath no temptation taken you but such as common to man: but God is faithful, who will not suffer you to be tempted above that ye are able; but with the temptation also make a way to escape, that ye may be able to bear it.***
>
> 1 Corinthians10:13

The bible recommend that you follow those who have obtained what you are striving to obtain. These are those who are examples, whom you respect; who have the kind of testimonies that you desire. One of the recommended ways is by going through the materials of others life story.

Study And Learn From Biographies

The Bible says:

> ***Now all these things happened unto for examples: and they were written for our admonition...***
>
> 1 Corinthians 10:11

One major way of being "*...followers of them who through faith and patience inherit the promises*" is through their biographies. These could be in a printed form such as a book; or it could be in an electronic form, audio or video.

A biography is the life story of a person written by

someone else. As a minister's wife, it is important for you to learn to study the biographies of others; especially ministers' wives who have excelled and thus have inherited the promises.

Why Biographies?

They provide examples to learn from because the secrets of men are in their stories. You must understand the secret of learning from examples if you want to get to God's destination for your life. History has a way of always repeating itself – negatively or positively. There are biblical and contemporary biographies for you to learn from.

The Bible is full of stories of those that either lost out of their destinies or those that made full proof of it. A few of these include the following:

Gehazi was Elisha's servant and heir apparent to the great unction and anointing upon Elisha's life and ministry. Unfortunately, he lost it all to Covetousness. The Bible gave this record in 2 Kings 5:20-27. Instead of becoming an anointed minister, he ended up as a notable leper.

Judas was one of Jesus' twelve disciples. Like the others, he walked and dinned with Jesus, but ended up betraying him due to covetousness (Matthew 26:14-16). He did not only end up a loser on earth, he will spend eternity in hell; because he did not repent before taking his own life. He ended in shame.

Delilah – In Judges 16:1-21 the bible gave a record of a lady that could have married God's servant and probably become one of the most referenced minister's wife. But she gave in to covetousness and sexual sin. She became an instrument in the hand of the devil. She was not spared; she died along side those that sent her.

David, the man after God's heart: with his whole heart he danced for the Lord (2 Samuel 6:14). He was a generous giver. He singlehandedly provided all that was needed for the building of the temple. Due to his constant enquiry from God, he never lost any battle. When he was caught up in a sin, he cried out for help and he was forgiven (2Samuel 12:13). He maintained his position in the heart of God. God established his throne forever. 2Samuel 7:16

When you study the lives of those who have gone ahead of you, you will be able to learn from them and avoid their pit falls.

In our contemporary world today, there are examples of men and women that are worth emulating. Find out about successful ministers and their wives, look out for their secrets, follow the secrets and you will become the next success story.

You can't become a story until you acquaint yourself with the stories of others who have obtained a good report. "Those who don't have references never become a reference": says my husband Dr. David Oyedepo. This is true! One tree never makes a forest.

Every man that is now a reference has had to identify with several references of men previously.

The Bible says:

> ***Hearken unto me ye that follow after righteousness, ye that seek the lord. Look unto me ye that follow after righteousness, ye that seek the lord. Look unto the rock whence ye are hewn, and to the hole of the pit whence ye are digged.***
>
> ***Look unto Abraham your father, and unto Sarah that bare you: for I called him alone, and blessed him, and increased him.***
>
> Isaiah 51:1-2.

As you look unto God, the rock from whence ye are hewn, you are also to look unto your father, Abraham. You are not to look only unto God but also unto the fathers who have gone ahead of us in the race.

As you look at their lives, you are able to interpret the scriptures correctly and to see farther. Wisdom demands that you stand on the shoulders of those who have gone ahead of you, and their stories are invaluable assets in achieving yours.

Your place will only be secured by the degree of illumination you carry. Time is precious and it is irrecoverable. Instructions are the pathway of wisdom. As you study the lives of those who have already inherited the promises, it becomes easy to wisely avoid mistakes that they made and pick instructions from what they did right.

Please be aware: you must however be discreet enough not to take everything you read or hear line, hook and sinker; rather, apply wisdom in knowing what to learn and what to unlearn by avoiding their mistakes.

I personally take delight in reading biographies of ministers and ministers' wives, especially those who have been in full time pulpit preaching ministry.

For instance, I have read books written by and the biographies of great men and women of God like T L and Daisy Osborn, Kenneth and Oretha Haggin, John G. lake, Archbishop & Bishop (Mrs.) Benson Idahosa, Kathryn Kuhlman, to mention but a few.

Remember, for you to see brighter, you need the shoulders of those who have gone before you. One major way of doing this is by going through their biographies. You can take advantage of that.

Seek And Receive Godly Counsel

Not to die in silence, you must learn how to seek and receive godly counsel. The Bible says:

> ***Where no counsel is, the people fall: but in the multitude of counselors there is safety***
>
> Proverbs 11:14

The first step to take when you are seeking godly counsel is to go to God himself. Open up to God; let Him know what you are going through. He is a very present help (Psalms 46: 1). Seek counsel from God first!

Seeking counsel from God requires you going through His word. Search the scriptures. Be filled with the knowledge of the word of God, let it dwell in you richly (Colossians 3: 16). This will help to balance any other form of counsel that you might receive.

Prayerfully let God lead you to the right person or persons to talk to. Everybody may not approach your issue with the right attitude or offer the right counsel, though; you must bear this in mind.

Seeking counsel from others, especially those that have gone ahead of you as a minister's wife is one of the ways through which you can raise your level of effectiveness.

However, your counselors must be carefully and prayerfully selected. Choose people with proven, tested and undeniable testimonies in the specific area where you desire to excel. Do not just seek counsel from someone that you know is struggling with a related issue.

Many today in the process of seeking counsel have compounded their problems. Apostle Peter told that lame man at the temple gate *...silver and gold have I none; but such as I have give I thee: ...* (Acts 3:6). Peter gave out of what he had and the man was made whole.

Do not expect anyone to give you what he does not have. For example, if your challenge is in the area of how to manage the ministry with your home front, you cannot receive practical and godly counsel from a divorced minister's wife. If you require counsel on effective financial management, it will be a disaster to approach someone who is involved in financial misappropriation for help.

Seek counsel from someone you respect, not one whose words you cannot obey. While Moses was leading the children of Israel through the wilderness, due to his lack of experience he almost wore himself out but for the counsel of his father in – law.

Jethro (Moses Father in – law) said:

> ***Harken now unto my voice, I will give thee counsel, and God shall be with thee... So Moses harkened to the voice of his father in - law, and did all that he had said.***
>
> Exodus 18:19a, 24.

Moses took to the advice of his father in law because he respected him and that counsel helped in his administration.

The Bible says:

> ***Without counsel purposes are disappointed: but in the multitude of counselors they are established.***
>
> Proverbs 15:22

Your good intentions might be frustrated if you do not have good counselors. Do not be frustrated, do not suffer unnecessarily. Be loaded with the word of God and be full of the Holy Spirit as you open yourself to counsels from men. Your glorious destinies shall not be erased!

Employ The Tool Of Observation

The importance of the tool of observation is clearly stated in this passage in the bible. Pay close attention as you read this passage.

> ***Those things which you have both learned, and***

received, and heard, and seen in me, do, and the God of peace shall be with you.

Philippians 4: 9 (emphasis mine)

It is one thing to look; it is another thing entirely to see! Truly, as the saying goes; many eyes look but very few see. One very good way of enjoying help so as not to die in silence is by observation.

One 'sin' that you are likely to commit when you are with your mentor is the sin of familiarity. When you are around your mentor(s), don't be carried away by their physical appearance or become so emotional that you forget the vital issues of your life.

As you travel to places, attend meetings; meet with your mentor(s), etc., one great way to learn fast is; to always be receptive. Pay very close attention to people's (especially ministers' wives) way of life, how they relate with people/family members, handle issues, talk etc. These provide a wealth of information for you that no lectures or teaching sessions can.

If there is any specific area where you require a change; pay rapt attention to such specific aspect of their lives. From my observations, for example; I discovered that wives of truly great men of God do not struggle for the pulpit with their husbands. I believe this is one of the reasons why they command such respect whenever they are called upon to minister. They simply function under the unction of their minister husband.

Such women do not have identity problem, they enjoy peace both at home with their husbands and in their various ministries. This has helped in no small measure in my style of operation; and today, the grace of God is finding greater expression in my life than ever! You too can enjoy all round rest, if you care to learn through observations.

Ask Relevant And Revealing Questions

One of the major reasons why many are dying in silence is because they assume so many things. Assumption usually breeds frustration.

A woman that is given to assuming many things for example would neither enjoy peace at home nor in ministry. Why should you assume when you have a mouth to ask? One of the reasons God gave you a mouth is so you can ask questions when necessary! The Bible says:

> ***For I will give you a mouth and wisdom, which all your adversaries shall not be able to gainsay nor resist.***
>
> Luke 21: 15

Your mouth is not just for eating and drinking, it is

a weapon of war! Even God does not encourage assumption. Despite the fact that He knows whatever you are passing through, He still expect you to ask necessary questions so you can receive clarifications. He said: *"For everyone that asketh receiveth!"* (Luke.11:10). If you do not ask, do not expect an answer.

Have you ever noticed that most miracles that Jesus performed during his earthly ministry were direct products of questions? The phrase: *"what would you want me to do for you"* was common place; and each one received what they asked.

The man at the temple gate in Acts chapter 3 had been there for years. That implies that Jesus had seen him in that state before, yet He did not heal him. May be he would have died lame were it not that mercy prevailed on that fateful day when Peter and John came to the temple for prayer.

There are some situations that require your asking, not just your look; even if you claim not to be the talking type, like this man at the temple gate!

Blind Bartimaeus on the other hand In Mark 10: 46-52 received his healing with violence, by crying out for mercy. As soon as he knew it was Jesus passing and He had solution to his problems, he began to cry out ceaselessly for help:

> ***Jesus, thou son of David, have mercy on me.***
>
> ***And many charged him that he should hold his peace: but he cried the more a great deal, Thou son of David, have mercy on me.***
>
> Mark 10: 47-48

Sure enough, he got his sight back!

Most of the miracles in the gospels were direct results of questions. When in doubt, ask the Holy Spirit "What must I do?" and whatever He instructs you to do, go ahead and do it. (John 2:5)

If you need clarification on an issue, do not sweep it under the carpet; make sure it is resolved. Ask your husband or someone more knowledgeable than you to throw more light into such areas. The issues you do not resolve now might be a problem tomorrow. Save yourself from carrying unnecessary burdens! Ask the Holy Spirit and you will hear His voice.

> ***And thine ears shall hear a word behind thee, saying, This is the way, walk ye in I, when ye turn to the right hand, and when ye turn to the left.***
>
> Isaiah 30:21

You shall not miss God's voice on any issue of your life.

Go For Impartation!

So as not to die in silence, one major way out is

through impartation. There are various ways by which you can receive impartation.

Hand laying Read with me what the bible says about hand laying in this passage:

> ***And Joshua the son of Nun was full of the spirit of wisdom; for Moses had laid his hand upon him...***
>
> Deuteronomy 34:9

Another way to "*...follow those who through faith and patience inherit the promises*" is by such vessels laying hands on you. When you identify any human vessel from which you desire transference of unction to function in a particular area of life and ministry, request for such vessels to personally lay hands on you.

There is transference of spirit and anointing via the laying on of hands. You can also request hand laying from your mentor(s). Whatever grace that you see at work in their lives that you desire will begin to work in your life too. Do not be ashamed to ask. Moses impacted Joshua with the spirit of wisdom and he was able to carry out his divine assignment of leading the children of Israel into the promise land.

Prophetic prayers. This is another way of receiving impartation.

Seek and ask to be prayed over by those ahead of you.

Take advantage of every opportunity at your disposal; ask to be prayed over by them.

You may also decide to give venison that will draw blessings out of them in prayer. Isaac blessed Jacob and the blessing stayed (Genesis 26:33).

Jesus also prayed for His disciples before He left them, He said: *I pray for them: I pray not for the world, but for them which thou hast given me; for they are thine...* (John 17: 9-22)

Anointing with oil. This is another way of receiving impartation. Please be aware that: pouring of anointing oil is not a religious rite but one of the channels of impartation and transference of the Spirit of God. David was anointed as King by the pouring of the anointing oil.

> ***Then Samuel took the horn of oil, and anointed him in the midst of his brethren: and the Spirit of the LORD came upon David from that day forward.***
>
> 1 Samuel 16:13

So, when you are anointed with oil, it is the Spirit of the Lord that comes upon you! What a mystery!

Other spiritual materials. You could also receive impartation through materials from your superiors. Especially if they are not easily accessible, you can partake of the spirit that is at work in their lives through their materials; printed and electronics. Get connected by faith and before you know it, you are already working in their steps.

Watch As You Pray

Apart from impartation, you can also enjoy help rather than die in silence through prayer and watching. The Bible clearly states:

> ***Call unto me, and I will answer thee, and show thee great and mighy things, which thou knowest not.***
>
> Jeremiah 33:3

The subject of prayer in your quest for help cannot be over emphasized. God is the only one that can give you help when other helps fail. As your heavenly father, He promised to answer whenever you call.

Remember the word of the Lord which says:

> ***Seek ye the Lord while he may be found, call ye upon him while he is near:***
>
> Isaiah 55:6

"Is God not there at all times?" You may ask. Yes, He is always near; but that is when you do not have alternatives in your heart. Many put God as second option. They rely more on the arm of flesh more than God. He will not heed your cry if you have alternatives. He will not come into that situation if you had already made up your mind on what to do.

God is a very present help in times of need. *(Psalms 46:1)* He also said in His word that: *he (referring to you and me now) shall call me(God) and I will answer him: I will be with him in trouble; I will deliver him and honour him.* (Psalms 91:15)

Alongside with your prayer, be sensitive to His voice. Prophet Habakkuk said:

> ***I will stand upon my watch, and set me upon the tower, and will watch to see what he will say unto me, and what I shall answer when I am reproved.***
>
> Habakkuk 2: 1

Prayer is a two way channel, do not just keep talking; wait also to hear from Him.

So, call on God in prayer; open up to Him: He knows what is best for you.

Sincere Self Examination

Another way out, so as not to die in silence is by conducting self-examination. The Psalmist said:

> ***Search me, O God, and know my heart: try me, and know my thoughts:***
>
> Psalms 139:23

Some of the problems that many ministers' wives encounter are self inflicted. If a self appraisal can be carried out from time to time, you will discover that you will have fewer problems to solve.

First, sit down and ask the Holy Spirit to reveal to you the areas that require attention in your life. Examine yourself first. Carry out an honest assessment of yourself from time to time. You are the best examiner of yourself.

Ask yourself: what is my motive for taking the steps that I take? Is it for my selfish gain or for the benefit of others and the kingdom of God? If your motives are pure, your life will be flooded with peace. But if otherwise you will not have peace. The absence of peace results into tensions in different areas of life.

Your approach to things, your attitudes, and your lifestyle as a whole must be constantly put under a check. Perhaps you got married before your husband became a minister; now that he is a minister, you must know that your approach to some things will have to change. You are now a leader, you cannot be reacting to things the way you used to.

Your lifestyle now has to reflect that of a leader. Do not over do things and always ask the Holy Spirit for every minute detail before you take any action.

It very important that you examine your spouse! Don't turn a blind eye when he makes wrong decisions, takes wrong steps, tells "half-truths" or acts in any questionable manner. You must remember that as his wife, you will partake of whatever consequences arise out of his unbecoming actions in future.

That is not to say you should 'guard' him 'hand and foot' though, suspecting and inspecting his every move; but be sensitive and with wisdom and prayer, point out your observations. This is more of a preventive measure but it is sure worth it.

If it is a situation that is beyond your ability to handle, do not hesitate to make it known to your mentor; or someone that you know your husband respects. Call for help when you are still in the position of being helped.

This explains why it is very important that you and your minister husband should have spiritual fathers and mentors. It is primarily for your safety, especially as a minister's wife! If you and your husband do not have yet, this is the best time to act!

Relevant And Edifying Books

The Bible says in Proverbs 26:20: *"where no wood is there the fire goeth out..."* You need the 'wood' of wisdom in order to overcome some of the overwhelming challenges that may come your way as a minister's wife. How do you gather the wood? One way is by reading relevant and edifying books. You need wisdom in every aspect of your life and ministry. If wisdom is lacking, there will be no bound to struggling. The Bible says:

> ***Wisdom* is *the principal thing;* therefore *get wisdom: and with all thy getting get understanding.***
>
> Proverbs 4:7

The primary thing that you must seek is wisdom. The wisdom of God precedes every other step to be taken. Seek wisdom from books that specifically address your situation. Specific areas of needs should be taken into consideration. Reading books is like taking your prescription. You cannot use the drug meant for back ache to treat common cold; it won't work.

You must be cautious in selecting the kind of books that you read. Be careful about the authors of those books because you contact the spirit of the author via their books. You must discern what you read by the Spirit of God. Do not just swallow any junk in the name of reading books.

Use the Weapon of Fasting

Not to die in silence, you must know how to use the weapon of fasting appropriately. The Bible says:

> ***Howbeit this kind goeth not out but by prayer and fasting.***
>
> Matthew 17:20

Sometimes, the disciples of Jesus were faced with an impossible situation. They were puzzled why they could not solve a 'common' problem of casting out a devil. When Jesus came He told them that this 'kind' of problem might not be solved but by prayer and fasting. There are some kinds of challenges that will require you to back up your prayer with fasting.

Fasting is not just a religious rite but a powerful weapon in the hand of the believer. Isaiah 58:6-9, 11 & 14 gives a description of what fasting is supposed to accomplish. Fast with an understanding that God is closer to you than you can ever imagine.

For you as a minister's wife, fasting is not optional; neither should it be reserved for the time when you have challenges. Fast to build up your spirit man.

There was a woman named Anna who gave herself to prayer and fasting in the temple at the time Jesus was dedicated. The Bible records:

> ***And there was one Anna, a prophetess, the daughter of Phanuel, of the tribe of Asher: she was of a great age, and had lived with a husband seven years from her virginity;***
>
> Luke 2:36

She spoke in the Spirit when she saw Jesus, born and delivered to the world.

If you want an unusual result, different from what you have ever experienced, then you need to do what you have never done before.

If you struggle to fast as a minister's wife, you need to ask the Holy Spirit to help you out. Fasting for your good and it has amazing benefits as stated in the book of Isaiah 58: 8-9, 11-12, and 14.

You stand a chance of carrying all the listed benefits in the above scripture if you couple your prayer with fasting. Remember, however that your fast does not change God; rather, it changes you!

Learn To Trust God.

Your absolute dependency on God is the foundation of every other step you take to get out of any predicament. The Bible says:

> ***If the foundations be destroyed what can the righteous do?***
>
> Psalms 11:3

Your foundation for getting anything from God is your faith and absolute trust in Him and His word.

> ***Jesus saith unto him, Go thy way; thy son liveth. And the man believed the word that Jesus had spoken unto him, and he went his way.***
>
> John 4:50

The woman with the issue of blood had an unfeigned faith in Jesus to the extent that all she desired was just a touch of His garment. Expectedly, she got her miracle!

> ***When she had heard of Jesus, came in the press behind, and touched his garment.***
>
> ***For she said, If I may touch but his clothes, I shall be whole.***
>
> ***And straightway the fountain of her blood was dried up; and she felt in* her *body that she was healed of that plague.***
>
> Mark 5:27-29

Trust God that He will help you; couple it with the understanding that He may decide to use people around you to help you out. Believe that He will perform what He stated in His word:

> ***The LORD hear thee in the day of trouble; the name of the God of Jacob defend thee;***
>
> *Send thee help from the sanctuary, and strengthen thee out of Zion;*
>
> Psalms 20:2

Maintain your trust in God, no matter the situation. Absolute dependency on the Holy Spirit is a must.

How Do You Show That You Trust God?

- Show confidence in His word

For verily I say unto you, Till heaven and earth pass, one jot or one tittle shall in no wise pass from the law, till all be fulfilled.

Matthew 5:18

- Take necessary action to back up your faith

Even so faith, if it hath not works, is dead being alone.

James 2:17

- Confess with your mouth the good report of God

Run now, I pray thee, to meet her, and say unto her, **Is it** ***well with thee?*** **is it** ***well with thy husband?*** **is it** ***well with the child? And she answered,*** **It is** ***well.***

2 Kings 4:26

- Do not draw back.

Now the just shall live by faith: but if **any man draw back,** ***my soul shall have no pleasure in him.***

Hebrews 10:38

As I conclude this chapter, please be reminded that God has a good and perfect thought for you. He said in His word concerning you:

For I know the thoughts that I think toward you, saith the LORD, thoughts of peace, and not of evil, to give you an expected end.

Jeremiah 29:11

The nuggets shared in this chapter are some of my greatest secrets in life and ministry. Apply them, and you will discover that you will not only be effective as a minister's wife, but you will become a pace-setter, a shining example from whom others can learn.

FOOD FOR THOUGHT

"A Problem shared is a problem solved."

Anonymous

Chapter 13

Take Heed

And say to Archippus, Take heed to the ministry which thou hast received in the Lord, that thou fulfill it.

Colossians 4:17

It is very crucial and important to always remember that being a minister's wife is a ministry from the Lord, it is an enviable position; whether you carry such a title or not. It is not accidental that you are a minister's wife. Therefore, it is not a position to be careless about.

It is a ministry that you have received from the Lord! However, it is one thing to receive a ministry from the Lord but another entirely to fulfill it. You have a responsibility therefore to take heed to your ministry as a minister's wife so you can fulfill it.

According to the *Oxford Advanced Dictionary*, to "take heed" means to note something carefully and act accordingly; to always be conscious or aware of something; to be careful to remember or be conscious of something.

God wants us to make a full proof of every ministry given to us. Apostle Paul in the bible said to Timothy and in essence to us all:

> ***But watch thou in all things, endure afflictions, do the work of an evangelist, make full proof of thy ministry.***
>
> 2 Timothy 4:5

What you have received is not in vain but you have a responsibility to make full proof of the ministry committed into your hands. Contrary to popular belief, ministry work is not for the lazy but for those that have a sense of direction and are ready to give it what it takes; irrespective of the challenges, so as to enjoy accomplishment.

Apostle Paul, as a minister also had challenges; but with all confidence, he said:

> ***But none of these things move me, neither count I my life dear unto myself, so that I might finish my course with joy, and the ministry, which I have received of the Lord Jesus, to testify the gospel of the grace of God.***
>
> Acts 20:24

From the above scriptures, it is clear that you as minister's wife have a responsibility to make full proof of, finish with joy and fulfill the ministry which the Lord has committed unto you.

How can this possibly be? You may ask. The Bible says:

> ***TAKE HEED to the ministry which thou hast received in the lord... that thou fulfil it.***
>
> Colossians 4:17

It is one thing to receive a ministry from the Lord but another entirely to fulfill it. That you are privileged to be a minister's wife does not guarantee automatic effectiveness and success.

There are principles to follow for you to fulfill your call. It is possible to receive a ministry from God and never fulfill it! Remember Judas: he was named among the twelve but he later lost out. Concerning him, the scripture says:

> ***Men* and *brethren, this Scripture must needs have been fulfilled, which the Holy Ghost by the mouth of David spake before concerning Judas, which was guide to them that took Jesus.***
>
> ***For he was numbered with us, and had obtained part of this ministry***
>
> ***...and his bishopric let another take.***
>
> Acts 1:16-17, 20

May your place not be taken by another!

In order for this ministry of being a minister's wife that you have received from the Lord to find fulfillment, you must "take heed", in other words: "note carefully and act accordingly, be conscious or aware of your given assignment".

Until you begin to take heed, your assignment as a minister's wife will not find fulfillment. It is a command from God to you to take heed, not an advice; and must be done on a continuous basis, not just periodically: if fulfillment is your goal.

How then, does one "take heed?" You may ask. Let's briefly examine how here.

Constant intake of the word of God

First, you take heed by a regular and constant intake of the word of God. Maintain a constant hunger and thirst for more of God's word, giving it priority place in your day-to-day affairs. God's word contains the thoughts of the Father concerning your life and ministry. It is a strengthener; it is the food that enables you to grow.

Both you and your minister husband should constantly keep yawning for spiritual growth. You need to constantly take in the word just as a baby takes inn milk. Concerning this, the scripture says:

> ***As newborn babes, desire the sincere milk of the word, that ye may grow thereby:***
>
> 1 Peter 2:2

Your study time is like the cooking time in the kitchen where you produce food that both you and others eat. It is beneficial also to document through writing, whatever God reveals to you during your time of study and indeed at all times.

This will enhance proper recall as at when needed later, to refresh both you and others. This is what I do personally, during all my study times and it is very helpful and refreshing.

Make the word of God your focus for living as a minister's wife. Whatever the word instructs, do it! Be a practitioner of what you hear, read, learn and preach. Thank God, the Holy Spirit is always present to bring to our remembrance what is learnt whenever it is required. Talking about the Holy Spirit, the Bible says:

> ***...He shall... bring all things to your remembrance, whatsoever I have said unto you,***
>
> John 14:26

However, the Holy Spirit can only remind you of what you have learnt, not what you don't know. This is the reason why you must saturate your heart with the word of God. Allow the word to dictate your way of life and the steps you take. Let the word dwell in you richly (Colossians 3: 16). Again, the Bible says:

> ***Thy word is a lamp unto my FEET, and a light unto my path.***
>
> Psalm 119: 105

God's word must be allowed to direct even your physical feet to where ever they should carry you to. There are places, for instance where you should never be found as a minister's wife. Places for instance where God's name is not glorified, or where other women gossip, where there is strife, envy and so on. These are places that if you keep going, could cause you to lose your placement in God's kingdom.

Constant word practice will also enable you discern the good from the evil. Your senses are trained to tune in to the spirit of God, you become spiritually sensitive. You cannot afford to remain a baby in the things of God. The scripture says:

> ***For every one that useth milk* is *unskillfull in the word of righteousness: for he is a babe.***
>
> ***But strong meat belongeth to them that are of full age,* even *those who by reason of use have their senses exercised to discern both good and evil.***
>
> Hebrews 5:13-14

You must train yourself to bend down to study the word, in season and out of season; when convenient and when difficult. Being busy is not an excuse for becoming word-dry.

You must create time out of your busy schedule to study the word through personal bible study, listening to tapes, reading of relevant books; among others. You can only walk by the light that you have contacted from the word of God.

God's word is the light of life that you require in your daily walk in this dark world. Therefore, it is: more word, more light and vice versa.

Maintain a fervent prayer life

Secondly, to take heed, you must know how to pray fervently. Your prayer closet is like your watch tower. In those days in the ancient cities, a tall building called 'tower' is usually erected close to the city wall. From this tower, a watch man watches out for any likely invasion of the enemy. He sounds an alarm by blowing the trumpet when necessary, to alert others.

Prayer is your medium of communication with your heavenly father; with it, you are in touch with the spirit world and are therefore able to gain command here on earth.

From your prayer room, you are able to see farther;

beyond what the physical eyes can, into the spiritual and thereby gain command. By it, unnecessary temptations and snares in life can be foreseen, avoided and overcome. This explains why the Bible says:

> ***Watch and pray that ye enter not into temptation...***
>
> Matthew 26:41

Studying the word is sowing the seed of the word into your heart. Prayer is the watering system with which the seed of the word require before it can germinate and bring forth fruits. The word is the seed and prayer is the watering system needed for the seed to grow.

Your constant word intake and fervent prayer life must grow at the same level; else it may result in spiritual lameness of some sort. This clearly explains why the scripture says:

> ***But we will give ourselves continually to prayer, and to the ministry of the word.***
>
> Acts 6: 4

The word of God and prayer are two things you must give yourself to; this will not happen on its own without your constant pressing, neither will it happen over-night!

To maintain a fervent prayer life, your prayer should

not be once a while or only when there are challenges; rather, it should be your normal way of life. On the subject of prayer, Jesus said:

> ***Men ought always to pray, and not to faint;***
>
> Luke 18:1

This becomes even more energizing and rewarding when you understand and practice how to pray in the Spirit; in other tongues, as the scriptures command (1Corinthians 14:2)! May your prayer life become revolutionized from this day on!

What Do You Gain By Maintaining A Fervent Prayer Life?

Let's examine some of them here, briefly.

Overcome Temptations

As a minister's wife, the peculiar situations with which you are confronted are basically spiritual and can therefore be adequately dealt with through prayer. You must learn to pray fervently for your husband, the family, the ministry, among others; consistently.

This will help ward off temptations and evil intentions of the wicked. Jesus told His disciples to pray so they do not fall into temptations (Matthew 26:41).

You Build Up Your Faith

The importance of prayer in building up your faith cannot be over-emphasized, especially when you pray in the Spirit-in tongues. The scriptures clearly states:

> ***But ye, beloved, building up yourselves on your most holy faith, praying in the Holy Ghost,***
>
> Jude 1:20

Praying in an unknown tongue is one of the weapons that can be used to confuse the devil and put him in total disarray. This is because when you pray in tongues, you are speaking mysteries unto God; to which the devil has no access.

> ***For he that speaketh in an unknown tongue speaketh not unto men, but unto God: for no man understandeth him; howbeit in the spirit he speaketh mysteries.***
>
> 1 Corinthians 14:2

Strength is imparted

The prayer room is the power room. Concerning our Lord Jesus, the Bible says:

> ***...and kneeled down and prayed saying Father ...and there appeared an angel unto him from heaven, STRENGTHENING HIM...****(emphasis mine).*
>
> Luke 22:41-43

There is a typical kind of strength that is available in prayers that enables you to face situations that come your way in a supernatural way. Even Jesus needed this kind of strength before He could face the cross; and thank God, He received it!

Direction

One other benefit you enjoy in prayer is divine direction. Since prayer is communication between you and God, it enables you to wait in His presence so as to receive instructions on where He is leading you on various specific issues of your life. The Bible says:

> ***And thine ears shall hear a word behind thee, saying, This is the way, walk ye in it, when ye turn to the right hand, and when ye turn to the left.***
>
> Isaiah 30:21

As you are aware, divine direction is constantly required in all areas of life in your decision making. When Apostle Paul was to be commissioned, they prayed, fasted and ministered unto the Lord; and then they received direction on the next step to take. The Holy Ghost spoke to the early church, read this account here:

> ***As they ministered to the Lord, and fasted, the Holy Ghost said, Separate me Barnabas and Saul for the work whereunto I have called them.***
>
> Acts 13:2

When you are in prayer, you cannot be in confusion; rather, you enjoy direction. Clearly, you are able to know what next step to take.

The subject of divine direction is so crucial because you will always require it; neither can you ever outgrow it.

You Are Refreshed

Obviously, time spent in the presence of the Lord in prayer are usually times of refreshing (Acts 3: 19). Prayer times are usually pleasurable and memorable. The scripture says:

> ***Thou wilt show me the path of life: in thy presence* is *fullness of joy; at thy right hand* there are *pleasures forevermore.***
>
> Psalms 16:11

When you know how to stand strong in prayer, rather than being stressed, you are refreshed!

Engage in diligent and faithful service

Thirdly, taking heed to the ministry that you have received from God as a minister's wife require you to be engaged in diligent and faithful kingdom service. Locate a place of service in the kingdom; do it diligently and faithfully.

To be faithful is to carry out service to God from your heart, with your best abilities; whether you are commended or not. Faithfulness is "doing what you are supposed to without supervision." Whether someone commends you or not, if your desire is seeing to it that the calling is fulfilled, then you are faithful. God always rewards the faithful. Read this scripture with me here:

> ***For God** **is not unrighteous to forget your work and labor of love, which ye have showed toward his name, in that ye have ministered to the saints, and do minister.***
>
> Hebrews 6:10

You cannot be fulfilled in ministry without faithfulness. God always looks for and rewards faithfulness. Therefore, 'take heed' be faithful in discharging all your various responsibilities.

Your responsibilities should also be carried out diligently. On the subject of diligence, the scripture says:

> ***Seest thou a man (woman) diligent in his/her business? He (she) shall stand before kings (queens) he (she) shall not stand before mean men (emphasis mine).***
>
> Proverbs 22:29

Diligence, that is: earnestness or zeal is required for you to see your ministry as a minister's wife fulfilled.

Without earnestness and zeal, your calling cannot be fulfilled. The Bible clearly states that:

> ***...he becometh poor that dealeth with a slack hand...***
>
> Proverbs 10:4

As daughters of Zion, we are exhorted:

> ***Let not thine hands be slack.***
>
> ***The LORD thy God in the midst of thee* is *mighty; he will save, he will rejoice over thee with joy; he will rest in his love, he will joy over thee with singing.***
>
> Zephaniah 3:16-17

This scripture is for you:

> ***...How long are ye slack to go to possess the land which the Lord God of your fathers hath given you?***
>
> Joshua 18:3

As you begin to take heed, you begin to bear more fruit which in turns brings you greater joy. The testimonies from others about the impact of your life on theirs give credence to the fact that you are taking heed to the ministry committed into your hands as a minister's wife.

The good news is: no matter how abundant the testimonies of your impact right now, there is room for much more! After all, the virtuous woman of **Proverbs 31** could see and hear of her impact and fruit bearing in the lives of others in her life time. You can too, if only you will 'TAKE HEED'!

FOOD FOR THOUGHT

"What matters now as always
is not what we can do:
it is what we can and must do."
Anonymous

Chapter 14
The Grace Factor

> ***But by the grace of God I am what I am: and his grace which* was bestowed *upon me was not in vain; but I labored more abundantly than they all: yet not I, but the grace of God which was with me.***
>
> 1 Corinthians 15:10

God is loving and understanding. He knows the frailty of our flesh and the inability of our natural ability to please Him. Haven gone through this material, perhaps you have being wondering how you can successfully carry out your assignment; or maybe you feel inadequate and not up to the daunting task ahead of you as a minister's wife; or you see yourself lacking in one area or the other.

Please be aware that God is not a wicked God. He will never demand from you what is beyond His grace in you, the price will never be greater than the available grace. He will never ask of you that which is beyond you, what you cannot do or that which will cause sorrow or be burdensome. The scripture says ...*and his commandments are not grievous,* (1 John 5:3).

However, He makes GRACE available to His children. His grace is always available when a task cannot be accomplished by human effort. To be a successful minister's wife is a possibility and the reason for this book is to enhance your effectiveness and fulfillment, thereby enabling you to shine brighter in your calling.

What is GRACE?

Grace is the divine enabling or power to accomplish a divine task or assignment, which is impossible by mere human effort. It is unmerited because it is freely given from the Lord to all that ask and receive it. It is not worked for, therefore cannot be purchased with money; but is to be received!

This grace is not for a select few, it is available to all; and you are included in the list! Concerning this, the scripture clearly states:

> ***For the grace of God that bringeth salvation hath appeared to all men,***
>
> Titus 2:11

This grace has appeared unto all men including you, it is therefore available; but it is your responsibility to tap into it.

The Source of Grace

If you need a particular thing, the first step to take is to go in search of the source, where it can be found; then get connected to it. When you are connected to the source of a thing, you can never lack that thing.

For instance, if you need water to cook, you do not go to your wardrobe in search of it, because your wardrobe is not connected to any source of water; rather, you go to your tap and open it so you can get as much as you need.

In the same vein, if you need grace as a minister's wife, you do not seek it from men; rather, you go to the source who is God. God is so kind and has made this grace available through His son Jesus Christ. This explains why the scripture says:

> ***...grace and truth came by Jesus Christ***
>
> John 1:17

God is the only authentic source of grace. He gave you the assignment and He knows the grace required to successfully carry it out.

Noah was called and given a special assignment, but he was not left unequipped; the bible said concerning him:

> ***But Noah found grace in the eyes of God.***
>
> Genesis 6:8

Just like Noah, you also can find grace in the sight of God. The subject of grace is so crucial; this is because without it, you are ill-equipped and may never fulfill your ministry!

Please be aware, grace has a genuine source; it comes from God through Jesus Christ. So, outside of Jesus Christ, you have no access to this grace.

Grace is a necessity, if effectiveness is your desire as a minister's wife. Also, grace can be stirred up, grow or frustrated. But, what makes grace a necessity? You may ask.

Why Do I Need Grace?

Being a minister's wife involves a lot of responsibility and giving. A lot is expected of you and at times your responsibilities may seem overwhelming and even tasking on you physically. At such times, all you need is to plug into the grace of God. Apostle Paul said in the scripture:

> ***And he said unto me, My grace is sufficient for thee: for my strength is made perfect in weakness. Most gladly therefore[3767] will I rather glory in my infirmities, that the power of Christ may rest upon me.***
>
> 2 Corinthians 12:9

To love

As a minister's wife, you will come in contact with a lot of people; some 'loveable', others 'un-loveable'. There are those who will even deliberately seek occasion to hurt you!

However, as a woman of vision on a mission; you have a commandment to love everyone. Jesus said:

> ***But I say unto you, Love your enemies, bless them that curse you, do good to them that hate you, and pray for them which despitefully use you, and persecute you;***
>
> ***That ye may be the children of your Father which is in heaven: for he maketh his sun to rise on the evil and on the good, and sendeth rain on the just and on the unjust.***
>
> Matthew 5:44-45

It is practically humanly impossible for you to fulfill this commandment without a constant baptism of God's grace.

To give

One of the most challenging areas of the office of a minister's wife is in giving. You must learn to practice liberality at all times. You will come in contact with many with various kinds of needs, expecting their needs to be met when they meet you. So, you really need

God's grace to be able to know what, how and when to give in wisdom with discretion.

Contrary-wise, some ministers' wives are mere collectors, expecting everyone they come across to give to them; sapping every available person around them without servicing any one's needs. This ought not to be so! God is a giving God, so you ought to give also! The Bible says:

> ***Give, and it shall be given unto you; good measure, pressed down, and shaken together, and running over, shall men give into your bosom. For with the same measure that ye mete withal it shall be measure to you again.***
>
> Luke 6:38

Worthy of note in the above scripture is the fact that only givers are qualified to receive. But to give acceptably, you require grace. This explains why the bible expressly talks about the giving grace (2Corinthians 8: 9). This grace is what makes giving stress-free and delightsome.

To intercede

Intercession is one of the life lines of a successful ministry. For you to be effective and make a remarkable impact in life and ministry, you must know how to stand in the gap and intercede for your minister husband, your home, the ministry and for the people.

The power that backs up the spoken word is from prayers. Most times it may not be convenient, but the scripture enjoins us not to faint **(Luke 18: 1).** The good news however, is that God's grace is always available to strengthen. The Bible says:

> ***I can do all things through Christ which strengtheneth me.***
>
> Philippians 4:13

To witness to others about Jesus

We are ambassadors of Christ and the great commission is to preach Christ to the end of the world. You cannot do this without grace.

> ***Go ye therefore, and teach all nations, baptizing them in the name of the Father,*** **and of the Son, and of the Holy Ghost:**
>
> ***Teaching them to observe all things whatsoever I have commanded you: and, lo, I am with you always, even unto the end of the world. Amen.***
>
> Matthew 28:19-20

As a minister's wife, you witness both by the words of your mouth and by your conduct. You are set up as a light so you must shine for others to glorify your heavenly father.

You cannot afford to be a reproach to the body of

Christ nor the ministry that God has given to your husband. However, this cannot be accomplished without the grace of God.

To run your home and the ministry

Your home as a minister's wife is your first mission field. Ministry begins from home (Acts 1:8). If you fail at the home front, then you have failed in the ministry. So, you need grace to keep the two running successfully.

In as much as the ministry needs your attention, never lose sight of the fact that your children and the entire family need you even much more. Consider for a moment the scripture that says:

> ***She looketh well to the ways of her household, and eateth not the bread of idleness.***
>
> ***Her children arise up, and call her blessed; her husband*** also, ***and he praiseth her.***
>
> ***Many daughters have done virtuously, but thou excellest them all.***
>
> Proverbs 31:27-29

Woman, you must look well to the ways of your household. Teach them the word of God and live same for them to see, let your life be a practical demonstration of what you teach.

When our children were still young and living with

us in our home, regular bible studies and prayer meetings were organized for them. Several times my husband, due to the demand of ministry work was not there; but I accepted the responsibility and made it a point of duty to teach them.

Today, I am so grateful to God and most fulfilled to see them walk in their destiny! Two of them are ordained ministers of the gospel, doing exploits with attendant undeniable proofs while the other two are shining examples in their academic pursuits.

Aside from our biological children, many who have been raised in our home are also doing well in their various life pursuits today. The Bible says:

> ***And all thy children* shall be *taught of the LORD; and great* shall be *the peace of thy children.***
>
> Isaiah 54:13

Until you begin to make impact in these areas, you have not begun to be effective. Now that you are aware of the areas where you require God's grace, you may be asking: how do I access this grace? How do you connect to the grace of God?

Simply Ask!

Now that you have a good understanding of the source of grace as well as the areas where you require it, the next thing you need to do is to just go ahead and do what Jesus commanded in His teachings on the mountain, He said:

> ***Ask, and it shall be given you; seek, and ye shall find; knock, and it shall be opened unto you:***
>
> ***For every one that asketh receiveth; and he that seeketh findeth; and to him that knocketh it shall be opened.***
>
> Matthew 7:7-8

The moment you identify the specific area where you require God's grace, go to Him in prayer; He shall bestow it upon you without measure. Learn to focus on God for an outpouring of grace to carry out your God-given assignment. You can call for a fresh supply of grace every single day. This has been my practice for the past many years, and I can boldly tell you: it does work!

Please be aware, the grace that God has bestowed upon you should not be allowed to be dormant or lie fallow; it should be activated, stirred up!

How to Stir up Grace

Before grace can produce and benefit you, you have a responsibility to stir it up. Except it is stirred up, it remains dormant and ineffective. Grace can be stirred up through:

Studying the scriptures

As a minister's wife, studying of the scripture is not an option, it is mandatory. If you must show yourself as an approved minister you must increase your knowledge of God. The Bible says:

> ***Grace and peace be multiplied unto you through the KNOWLEDGE of God and our saviour Jesus Christ***
>
> 2 Peter 1:2

As your knowledge of God increased, so also will His grace increase and multiply in your life.

Giving yourself to kingdom service

In every probability, one could be carried away with the thinking of being in the main stream of kingdom service as a minister's wife because of the office you occupy. However, you must be aware that occupying an office is not synonymous with being in service.

Ensure that you consciously give yourself to kingdom service in whatever capacity God enables you, with a right heart. Acceptable service must come from the heart.

Amaziah, one of the kings in Israel rendered service unto God; most likely, men would have commended him. But as far as God was concerned, his service was not acceptable because it was not with the right heart.

Read this report:

> ***Amaziah* was *twenty and five years old* when *he began to reign, and he reigned twenty and nine years in Jerusalem. And his mother's name* was *Jehoaddan of Jerusalem.***
>
> ***And he did* that which was *right in the sight of the LORD, but not with a perfect heart.***
>
> 2 Chronicles 25:1-2

Render service from the heart; let your heart be involved in whatever you do. Remember, God is not a respecter of persons. For further enlightenment concerning kingdom service, you can get a copy of my book titled: Service-The Master Key.

When you are divinely enabled, you are on the path of effectiveness as a minister's wife; precious in the sight of God and valued by men. Like Apostle Paul, you will be able to say: *...by the grace of God I am what I am...* (1Corinthians 15:10.)

So, I say unto you: 'TAKE GRACE NOW! to become what God has called you to be! - an effective minister's wife.

Growing In Grace

One unique thing about the grace of God is that it is not stagnant or static. It can increase and be multiplied, you can grow in it!

Remember that stagnant water stinks, so ensure that you put the grace of God upon your life to work so that it does not get stale or stink. There are some ministers' wives today who only talk about 'the good old days', because the grace of God has been taken for granted and has become stale. Do not frustrate the grace of God upon you.

> ***I do not frustrate the grace of God: for if righteousness* come *by the law, then Christ is dead in vain.***
>
> Galatians 2:21

Why Grow In Grace?

Like every other spiritual endowments, the grace of God can be frustrated and made void when it is abused in any way. There is need for you to keep step with Jesus in your daily walk, appropriating His grace judiciously and with all integrity. You need to grow in grace among other things because:

It makes men

The scripture says:

> ***But by the grace of God I am what I am: and his grace which* was bestowed *upon me was not in vain;***

but I labored more abundantly than they all: yet not I, but the grace of God which was with me.

1 Corinthians 15:10

Like Paul acknowledged in the above scripture, you cannot amount to anything in life outside of God's grace.

To become anything in life you need His grace! Truth is, we are whatever we are by the grace of God as there are no truly self-made people in this kingdom!

It conveys salvation

"Salvation" is a comprehensive word which encompasses your desires and fulfillment spirit, soul and body. So when you grow in grace, it translates to growth and progress in every department of your life. This is why the scripture says:

For the grace of God that bringeth salvation hath appeared to all men,

Titus 2:11

It delivers

Just like it is with Noah's example, the grace of God delivers from the floods of life; no matter what it is. Read this scripture with me:

And, behold, I, even I, do bring a flood of waters upon the earth, to destroy all flesh, wherein is the

> ***breath of life, from under heaven;* and *every thing that* is *in the earth shall die.***
>
> Genesis 6:17

Nothing can stop the grace of God at work in the life of a believer, especially ministers of the gospel; who is taking the lead in plundering the kingdom of darkness.

It makes the impossible possible

The grace of God turns impossibilities to possibilities. Noah was given a seemingly impossible task, yet it was accomplished by the instrumentality of grace. Read the record here:

> ***Make thee an ark of gopher wood; rooms shalt thou make in the ark, and shalt pitch it within and without with pitch.***
>
> ***And this* is the fashion *which thou shalt make it* of: *The length of the ark* shall be *three hundred cubits, the breadth of it fifty cubits, and the height of it thirty cubits.***
>
> Genesis 6:14-15

Humanly speaking, Noah's mission to build an ark against a flood was not sane, especially because it had never rained before! Yet, the grace of God made it possible and bailed him out; the same can happen for you.

How To Grow In Grace

If it is so important to grow in grace, how do I go about it? You may ask. Let us examine this here:

Live the Word

Genuine word practice is the only security for your redemption as well as your profiting.

> ***Grace and peace be multiplied unto you through the knowledge of God, and of Jesus our Lord,***
>
> 2 Peter 1:2

Be addicted to live the word of God. Let the word of God determine your life style. Become a word practitioner and not just a word hearer, preacher or teacher. Only word doers enjoy God's blessing and withstand the challenges of life (Matthew 7: 24 -27).

Make it a point of duty to consciously practice godliness. Remember: non-word-doers are self deceivers (James 1: 22)!

Guard your conscience

Your conscience is your God ordained policeman on earth; the scripture describes the duty of your conscience this way:

> ***Which show the work of the law written in their hearts, their conscience also bearing witness, and***

> **their *thoughts the mean while accusing or else excusing one another;***
>
> Romans 2:15

Listen to your conscience. Don't sear or kill it by deliberatly ignoring its nudging. Be conscience sensitive in all your dealings. Don't defile your conscience in any way, as this will definitely grieve the Holy Spirit.

Quench not the Holy Spirit

To grow in grace, you need the enabling of the Holy Spirit. The scripture says:

> ***But ye shall receive power, after that the Holy Ghost is come upon you:***
>
> Acts 1:8a

However, the Holy Spirit can be grieved and quenched. The scripture warns against this. It says: *Quench not the Spirit* (1 Thessalonians 5:19).

Wisdom demands that you dissociate from everything that can grieve or quench Him in your life, especially sin in any guise.

Beware of the relationships you keep

Disconnect from those who are not ready to grow in grace and are not committed to living a life of godliness like you are! Be reminded:

He that walketh with wise* men *shall be wise: but a companion of fools shall be destroyed.

Proverbs 13:20

Don't forget that relationships matter a lot, as they determine how well and how far you go in life and ministry. Choose your friends and ministry associates wisely.

With these, I see the grace of God multiply upon your life; making you more effective as a minister's wife and leaving an impact that cannot be erased, in Jesus name!

Welcome to your next level of greater effectiveness in life and ministry!

FOOD FOR THOUGHT

"The price is not greater than God's grace."

Oretha Hagin

Final Word

A Word To The Ministers

> ***...her husband* also, *and he praiseth her. Many daughters have done virtuously, but thou excellest them all.***
>
> Proverbs 31:29

This in closing is an admonition to the ministers of the gospel. You need to understand that your wives are a God-given treasure house, loaded with unique graces and abilities that can help you as well as boost the work of the ministry that God has committed into your hands.

Therefore, do not relegate your wife to the background in the work of the ministry. It is important that you give her every encouragement necessary, so she can correctly occupy her God-given position; to be BY YOUR SIDE.

Your wife is meant to be a help meet indeed to you. The Bible says:

And the LORD God said, It is not good that the man should be alone; I will make him a help meet for him.

Genesis 2:18

Please be aware: whether she looks like it or not, God has loaded your wife with virtues, graces and talents which if allowed her to manifest, will add to you as an individual and to the work God has committed into your hands. So let her be what God destined her to be.

Your wife should be your best friend and confidant in ministry; that is her God-given place! God is not interested in working with and through solo ministers; He works more effectively with husband and wife in ministry, as teammates. This is the wisdom of God for the end time. It makes for stability. The Bible says:

Two **are** ***better than one; because they have a good reward for their labor.***

Ecclesiastes 4:9

This is because this end time, God is set to show the world His many- sided wisdom; in all its infinite variety and innumerable aspects. Women too have a contribution to make in the display of this wisdom of God, being created also in God's image.

There is an aspect of God, the display of which is peculiar to minister's wives; which has been hidden for lack of opportunity to perform. When two are in agreement, they will always accomplish more than they would have individually. Jesus said:

> ***Again I say unto you, That if two of you shall agree on earth as touching any thing that they shall ask, it shall be done for them of my Father which is in***
>
> Matthew 18:19

Obviously, not all ministers' wives may be called to have a pulpit ministry; but all are called to stand by their husbands. Your wife has a God-ordained key role to play in the success of your life and ministry.

Take the wisdom step of investing in her: academically (if there is need), through relevant exposure, tireless encouragement and so forth. Every investment in this regard is worth it and will definitely yield great dividends for you and for the ministry. Correct her when she makes mistakes, lovingly; believe and invest in her. Lovingly and prayerfully deal with any sore issues in your relationship with her.

Seek counsel when and where necessary; whatever you do, co-operate with God to allow her take her place by your side. If you do not lovingly carry her along now, she may become a burden to you and to the work tomorrow.

Never forget that by and large, she is one flesh with

you. When everyone else is gone, the crowds no more there and the applaud fades; she is the one who will still be there with you.

Remember, your wife is Mrs. "You". She reflects you wherever she goes! As you make her to occupy her God – given place in your life and ministry, watch and see how you also will begin to enjoy greater peace of mind in the pursuit of your God-given vision and ministry. When she is by your side, you are for sure on your path to excellence!

This is God's divine arrangement and order; and you in particular should be willing to let God have His way in your marriage and ministry. As you do this, I see you making greater impact on a continuous basis!

SAILING UNDER SEALED ORDERS

12/9/76

Where, I do not know!

When, I cannot say!

Why, is not my business and How, must not concern me, but It is mine to accept from Him the sealed orders containing His blueprint for my life, and to open and read them just when and just as much as a time as He wills.

It is saying an eternal "Yes" to God. And eternal "No" to self.

"Lord, what will thou have me to do? Where will thou have me to go?

Having definitely relingquished all claims I deliberately turn my back on everything. Thus I renounce all that I am and have.

It's no longer mine but God's.

Henceforth, He has the absolute right to do what he like with it, and if at any time he should call upon me to literally forsake what I have renounced I must not even murmur or complain.

He must be Lord of all, or not Lord at all.

ABOUT THE AUTHOR

FAITH ABIOLA OYEDEPO HAS BROUGHT HOPE, JOY, AND LIFE INTO MANY HOMES IN HER GENERATION.

Having received a ministry for family and homes, she has dedicated her life to showing people God's perfect will for their homes and family relationships. Her weekly newspaper and internet columns: Family Matters, Family Success and Family Life have helped in no small way in achieving this goal.

She has shown in practical terms and through deep spiritual insight that the home can be the Eden God created it to be.

She has a divine mandate to make her shoulders available and enrich the lives of singles in a unique way.

Pastor Faith has written more than 12 books, including: Marriage Covenant, Making Marriage Work, Raising Godly Children, and her best selling title: Rescued From Destruction.

An anointed preacher of the gospel, Pastor Faith Abiola Oyedepo has been doggedly supportive of her husband (Dr. David o. Oyedepo, the Visioner and President of Living Faith Church Worldwide Inc.) in the daunting work of the ministry.

She has four children – David Jnr., Isaac, Love and Joys.

Books Authored by Faith A. Oyedepo

The Effective Minister's Wife

Single With A Difference

Rescued From Destruction

Making Marriage Work

Marriage Covenant

Raising Godly Children

You Can Overcome Anxiety

The Dignity Of The Believer

A Living Witness

Communion Table

Nurturing The Incorruptible Seed

Service: The Master Key

Stirring Up The Grace Of God

Building A Successful Family

The Spirit of Faith

Visit our website for weekly articles by the author:

http://www.davidoyedepoministries.org